Parents, Prodigals, and Prayers

31 day Devotional

ILYNMW Publishing
Atlanta Georgia

Paul Beersdorf

Copyright Paul Beersdorf 2026

paulbeersdorf@gmail.com

Published by: ILYNMW Publishing

V10.0

All rights reserved. No part of this publication may be reproduced, stored in a retrieval system, or transmitted in any form or by any means – electronic, mechanical, photocopy, recording, or any other – except for brief quotations in reviews, without the prior written permission of the publisher

Any Internet address, phone numbers, or company or product information printed in this book are offered as resources and are not intended in any way to be or to imply an endorsement by ILYNMW Publishing, nor does ILYNMW Publishing vouch for the existence, content, or services of these sites, phone numbers, companies or products beyond the life of this book.

"Scripture taken from the NEW AMERICAN STANDARD BIBLE®, Copyright © 1960,1962,1963,1968,1971,1972,1973,1975,1977,1995 by The Lockman Foundation. Used by permission."

During the writing of the book, the author used Google Gemini and Grammarly to help with chapter content, ideation, style, grammar and structure.

Cover Design: Paul Beersdorf

ISBN 978-1-971344-00-3

Books by Paul Beersdorf

- Flowers on Tuesday
- 52 Things I Wish My Father Had Told Me about Marriage and Family
- The 100 Most Important Words
- Encouraging Your Wife
- Encouraging Your Husband
- Advice for Today, Tomorrow and Forever
- Even Moses Needed Encouragement
- Storm Management
- Living Intentionally
- Luck, Chance or Prayer
- Choosing to Finish Well
- Destination – Dad 2.0
- Characteristics of a Leader
- Unleadership
- Devotional – The Character of God

Paul Beersdorf

Table of Contents

Dedication		Page 6
Introduction		Page 7
Our Story		Page 9
Praying Scripture		Page 12
Tough Prayers		Page 24
Good Company		Page 25
Famous Prodigals		Page 30
Character of God		Page 32
Day 1	The Loss	Page 39
Day 2	Be Still	Page 43
Day 3	Don't Give Up	Page 49
Day 4	Don't Give In	Page 55
Day 5	Life Goes On	Page 61
Day 6	Be at Peace	Page 66
Day 7	Take Every Thought Captive	Page 72
Day 8	Seek Wise Counsel	Page 77
Day 9	Beware of Bitterness & Envy	Page 83
Day 10	Fellowship	Page 89
Day 11	Friends	Page 94
Day 12	Family	Page 99
Day 13	Self-Control	Page 104
Day 14	Serving Others	Page 109
Day 15	Empathy	Page 114
Day 16	Vulnerability	Page 119
Day 17	Influence .vs Control	Page 124
Day 18	God's Promises	Page 129
Day 19	God's Comfort	Page 134
Day 20	Trusting God	Page 139
Day 21	Hope	Page 144
Day 22	When the answer is no	Page 149
Day 23	Your Role	Page 154
Day 24	Marathon	Page 159
Day 25	Timing	Page 164
Day 26	Why Pray	Page 170
Day 27	When to Pray	Page 174
Day 28	How to Pray	Page 178
Day 29	Where to Pray	Page 182
Day 30	Forgiveness	Page 186
Day 31	Your Identity	Page 191

Paul Beersdorf

Table of Contents

Epilogue	Page	196
Summary	Page	198
Final Thoughts	Page	207

Dedication

This book is dedicated to my beautiful Bride Debbie! You have walked by my side for these 35+ years and I am grateful and blessed to call you my best friend.

I love you no matter what!
You are the love of my life!
You are my best friend ever seen!
All of me loves all of you!
You are the only one for me!
You are the desire of my heart!
You captivate my heart!
You complete me and make me a better man!
If I had to choose all over again, I would choose you!
Thanks for saying yes!
I choose you!
143

Introduction

If you are reading this, then either you picked up this book because you have a prodigal child (or multiple prodigal children), or someone who loves you gave you this book. Either way, I am grateful and blessed that you have this book in your hands (or electronically as an eBook).

This is a tough journey!

How do I know this is a tough journey?

I know, because we have been on this journey since 2014 with a prodigal son and with two prodigal daughters in more recent years. Of our four children, three of them are prodigals. They have walked away from their faith, they have walked away from our family and they have walked away from the values and principles that they were raised upon.

So, yes I know it is a tough journey!

However, before we go further, I just want to acknowledge that God is good all the time and all the time God is good! He has walked with us through these trials and tribulations, and we believe God will redeem our children.

We believe God will refresh, restore and renew our family and use us for His kingdom work and ultimately bring honor and glory to Him.

The intent of this book is to encourage you and equip you for the road ahead. It might be short journey or it might be a journey of decades.

Either way, know that you are not alone, and certainly not the only one who is walking this path.

What you will not find in this book is some pithy three point plan or quick solution.

If I have learned anything, it is that God is sovereign and I cannot command His timing.

Finally, even though I don't know you, I have been praying for you and your family.

I have been praying for all parents of prodigals and their extended family members who might pick up and read this book.

I have also been praying that your prodigal will return soon.

Blessing to you!

Our Story

I was going to write a chapter about our story, but as I worked on this book, I did not want our story to be the driving narrative. Instead let me share some of the words and actions that have defined our journey in a very raw and vulnerable way.

Negatives (the beginning of the journey)

Anger
Broken heart (we still have broken hearts)
Disappointment
Depression
Sadness
Grief
Hopeless
Helpless
Disbelief
Pain
Shame
Embarrassment
Frustration
Wavering faith
Envy – over friend and family who have successful children
Bitterness

Positives (where we are now – but we still have bad days!!)

Surrender
Joy
Peace
Hopeful
Deep empathy for other families on this journey
More clarity about what we really believe
Closer relationship with God – deeper faith, deeper walk, deeper prayer
Closer relationship with my Bride
Ability to serve other families

We are not perfect and still have days when the negatives can creep in if we are not careful and guarding our hearts and minds.

I wanted to share this list because as we have interacted with so many families with prodigals we know they are struggling with the negative emotions and actions and can feel isolated and guilty because they think they are the only ones who are feeling this way.

The challenge for all of us as Christians is to move as quickly as we can through the negative emotions and actions and progress to a positive and productive walk with Christ.

To be clear; our journey in the negatives was much longer than we would have desired (not days or months, but years). Please know that one of the reasons we were in the negatives for so long was because we did not have anyone to come along side of us on this journey. At the time we did not know any families who were struggling with prodigals.

That is why we strive to help other families today. That is why I am writing this book. We want to encourage you to have a closer, deeper and more meaningful walk with God – even though your circumstances with your prodigal might not change as quickly as you desire.

Here are some quick things we have learned.

Things I cannot do!

I cannot change my prodigal
I cannot choose for my prodigal
I cannot control my prodigal
I cannot corral my prodigal
I cannot confuse my feeling with facts
I cannot enable them in their bad choice and decisions
I cannot fix them
I cannot live in the past
I cannot blame myself for their choices

Things I can do!

I can love them no matter what!
I can fully surrender them to God
I can pray for them

Things I can do!

I can praise God for them
I can communicate with them
I can challenge them
I can be concerned for them
I can offer tough love
I can ask others to pray for them
I can ask others to speak into their live
I can pray for divine encounters
I can hope for their future
I can be thankful for any good character qualities they have

When they awakened and come to their senses & ready for change then:

I can welcome them home
I can comfort them
I can offer mercy and grace
I can offer forgiveness
I can help them with recovery and restoration

One of our favorite family movies is a true story about a young man named Rudy who wanted to play football at Notre Dame. The movie is self-titled "Rudy". There is a scene in the movie when Rudy is in the chapel and praying over his situation (he was still not an official member of the team).

The wise Priest tells him a deep theological truth.

This is what he says: "In my 30 years of theological study, I have found only two incontrovertible truths – there is a God and I am not Him".
(Father Cavanaugh, *Rudy*, 1993)

I love that quote because it keeps me grounded in my own expectations and the things I can control (my attitude and actions) and the things outside my control.

As you read the rest of the book, take your time, take notes and share with your other family members your thoughts.

I hope by the end, you will have a closer walk with God and will be encouraged. Blessing to you!

Praying Scripture

The great thing about prayer is that your prodigal cannot stop you from praying for them! It does not matter what they believe, want or desire. You can take the greatest offensive weapon we have in our arsenal (The Bible) and wrap your prayers in the scripture and promises of God.

Speaking His Word: 50 Scriptures to Pray Over Your Prodigal

When you've tried everything and the fear is overwhelming, you need to remember that while your voice may tremble, God's Word does not ever tremble.

Your most powerful act is to take the very promises and truths God has revealed and pray them directly back to Him over your child and or children.

This chapter gives you 50 unshakeable anchors — specific verses from the Bible to use as your prayer guide.

When you pray scripture, you are confident that you are praying exactly in line with God's perfect will. All of these verses may not resonate with you or your situation, so take the time to curate those key verses that you believe will be the most effective and purposeful for your situation.

One thing I do is keep a list of the verses in the notes section of my phone so that they are easy to reach and read. This comes in handy when I find myself with time on my hands (waiting for someone or something), or even in the middle of the night when I wake and cannot fall back to sleep.

The Guide: How to Pray These Verses

<u>Make it Personal</u>: Don't just read the verse. Insert your child's name (or the words "my child") directly into the prayer.

Example (2 Peter 3:9): "Lord, I pray that [Child's Name] will know that You are not slow about Your promise, but are patient toward them, not wishing for [Child's Name] to perish, but for them to come to repentance."

<u>Pray with Authority</u>: Pray these words with the confidence that you are handling the ultimate weapon of spiritual warfare: the living Word of God.

<u>Focus on God's Action</u>: Notice that many of these prayers ask God to do something to your child's heart, mind, or circumstances, which only He can control.

Finally, don't forget as you pray to also praise God and thank God. This may be difficult and seem counterintuitive given the tough situation you are in, but my favorite set of verses in the Bible (my "life verses") are:

1 Thessalonians 5:16-18
Rejoice always,
Pray without ceasing,
in everything give thanks; for this is the will of God for you in Christ Jesus.

These three short verses have been my guide though many tumultuous trials and tribulations with my prodigal children. The verse does not say to be thankful "for" everything; it says to be thankful "in" everything! This is about my attitude in this situation.

Do I always succeed in following these three verses in the most difficult moments?

No of course not.

I am only human and frail and fragile at times. But I can say that I do quickly come around and come back to these verses. My goal is to reduce the amount of time it takes me to go from pain to praise and thanksgiving.

I. Praying for Repentance and Salvation (The Call Home)

These verses focus on the deepest desire: your child's spiritual safety and their return to a right relationship with God.

2 Peter 3:9: "The Lord is not slow about His promise, as some count slowness, but is patient toward you, not wishing for any to perish, but for all to come to repentance."

Prayer Focus: Pray for God's patience to continue pursuing your child and for their heart to be opened to repentance today.

2 Timothy 2:25-26: "if perhaps God may grant them repentance leading to the knowledge of the truth, and that they may come to their senses and escape from the snare of the devil, having been held captive by him to do his will."

Prayer Focus: Ask God to grant repentance and for your child to "come to their senses" (like the prodigal son) and escape the enemy's trap.

Romans 10:13: "for 'WHOEVER WILL CALL ON THE NAME OF THE LORD WILL BE SAVED.'"

Prayer Focus: Pray for the circumstances to align so that your child reaches a point of desperation and calls out to Jesus for help.

John 6:44: "No one can come to Me unless the Father who sent Me draws him; and I will raise him up on the last day."

Prayer Focus: Pray that the Holy Spirit would actively draw your child toward Jesus right now, breaking through every barrier.

Ezekiel 36:26: "Moreover, I will give you a new heart and put a new spirit within you; and I will remove the heart of stone from your flesh and give you a heart of flesh."

Prayer Focus: Ask God to perform the surgical miracle of replacement: remove the "heart of stone" and give your child a soft, responsive "heart of flesh."

Psalm 51:10: "Create in me a clean heart, O God, And renew a steadfast spirit within me."

Prayer Focus: Pray for God to create a clean heart and to restore a steadfast spirit so they do not continue to wander.

Ephesians 1:18: "I pray that the eyes of your heart may be enlightened, so that you will know what is the hope of His calling, what are the riches of the glory of His inheritance in the saints,"

Prayer Focus: Pray for the "eyes of their heart to be enlightened" to see the truth and the genuine hope of Christ.

II. Praying for God's Protection and Intervention (The Hedge)

These prayers ask God to intervene directly in your child's life and environment, protecting them from harm and destructive influences.

Psalm 91:11: "For He will give His angels charge concerning you, To guard you in all your ways."

Prayer Focus: Ask God to command His angels to guard your child from physical harm, especially when they are making dangerous choices.

Proverbs 3:6: "In all your ways acknowledge Him, And He will make your paths straight."

Prayer Focus: Pray that your child, in their confusion, would acknowledge God in some small way, allowing God to begin straightening their crooked path.

Psalm 139:7-8: "Where can I go from Your Spirit? Or where can I flee from Your presence? If I ascend to heaven, You are there; If I make my bed in Sheol, behold, You are there."

Prayer Focus: Pray that your child feels the relentless presence of God no matter how far they run. Pray they cannot escape His love.

2 Corinthians 4:4: "in whose case the god of this world has blinded the minds of the unbelieving so that they will not see the light of the gospel of the glory of Christ, who is the image of God."

Prayer Focus: Ask God to remove the spiritual blindness placed by the enemy so they can finally see the light of the Gospel.

Luke 8:12: "Those beside the road are the ones who have heard; then the devil comes and takes away the word from their heart, so that they will not believe and be saved."

Prayer Focus: Pray that God would protect the seeds of truth that have been planted in their heart, preventing the enemy from stealing the Word away.

1 Corinthians 15:33: "Do not be deceived: 'Bad company corrupts good morals.'"

Prayer Focus: Pray specifically for God to break the ties of bad company and remove toxic, destructive influences from their life.

Psalm 34:17: "The righteous cry and the Lord hears, And rescues them out of all their troubles."

Prayer Focus: Pray for the day your child cries out to God, and for God to rescue them from the troubles they are facing.

Deuteronomy 31:6: "Be strong and courageous, do not be afraid or tremble at them, for the Lord your God is the one who goes with you. He will not fail you or forsake you."

Prayer Focus (for the Parent): Pray this for your own courage when you fear your child's enemies or circumstances.

III. Praying for Wisdom and Clarity (The Mind)

These prayers ask God to renew your child's thinking, give them wisdom, and clarify their path.

James 1:5: "But if any of you lacks wisdom, let him ask of God, who gives to all generously and without reproach, and it will be given to him."

Prayer Focus: Pray that your child, in their confusion, would be driven to ask God for wisdom, and that God would grant it generously.

Romans 12:2: "And do not be conformed to this world, but be transformed by the renewing of your mind, so that you may prove what the will of God is, that which is good and acceptable and perfect."

Prayer Focus: Pray for the renewing of their mind, breaking conformity to the world and leading them to see God's good, acceptable, and perfect will.

Philippians 4:8: "Finally, brethren, whatever is true, whatever is honorable, whatever is right, whatever is pure, whatever is lovely, whatever is of good repute, if there is any excellence and if anything worthy of praise, dwell on these things."

Prayer Focus: Pray that your child's attention would be redirected toward things that are true, honorable, and pure, shifting their focus away from destructive thoughts.

Proverbs 4:18: "But the path of the righteous is like the light of dawn, That shines brighter and brighter until the full day."

Prayer Focus: Pray that God would begin to light their path one step at a time, leading them out of darkness and into increasing clarity.

Psalm 119:105: "Your word is a lamp to my feet And a light to my path."

Prayer Focus: Pray that God would use His Word (a book, a sign, a sermon) to light the next step your child needs to take.

Colossians 2:8: "See to it that no one takes you captive through philosophy and empty deception, according to the tradition of men, according to the elementary principles of the world, rather than according to Christ."

Prayer Focus: Pray that God would protect them from empty deception and damaging philosophies that have taken them captive.

Psalm 32:8: "I will instruct you and teach you in the way which you should go; I will counsel you with My eye upon you."

Prayer Focus: Pray for God's gentle instruction and counsel to reach your child, guiding their actions with His watchful eye.

IV. Praying for Restoration and Hope (The Future)

These verses are for your endurance and confidence, reminding you that God specializes in resurrection and restoration.

Proverbs 22:6: "Train up a child in the way he should go, Even when he grows older he will not abandon it."

Prayer Focus: Thank God for the seeds you planted and pray for the divine guarantee that your child will not abandon the truth forever.

Romans 8:28: "And we know that God causes all things to work together for good to those who love God, to those who are called according to His purpose."

Prayer Focus (for the Parent): Claim the promise that God is actively causing even this painful situation to work for good in your life and your child's life.

Lamentations 3:22–23: "The Lord's lovingkindnesses indeed never cease, For His compassions never fail. They are new every morning; Great is Your faithfulness."

Prayer Focus: Thank God that His mercies are new every single morning, giving your child a fresh chance and you fresh hope today.

Psalm 126:5: "Those who sow in tears shall reap with joyful shouting."

Prayer Focus: Acknowledge your tears (your sorrowful sowing) and claim the joyful shouting of a future harvest and restoration.

Joel 2:25: "Then I will repay you for the years Which the swarming locust has eaten, The crawling locust, the consuming locust, and the cutting locust, My great army which I sent among you."

Prayer Focus: Pray for God's power to restore the years and opportunities that have been lost to destructive choices.

Psalm 40:2: "He brought me up out of the pit of destruction, out of the miry clay, And He set my feet upon a rock, making my footsteps firm."

Prayer Focus: Pray that God would lift your child out of the "pit of destruction" and set their feet on the firm ground of Christ.

Jeremiah 29:11: "For I know the plans that I have for you,' declares the Lord, 'plans for welfare and not for calamity to give you a future and a hope.'"

Prayer Focus: Pray for God's good plans for a future and a hope to break through the enemy's plans of calamity and destruction.

Isaiah 61:7: "Instead of your shame, you will have a double portion, And instead of humiliation they will shout for joy over their portion. Therefore, they will possess a double portion in their land, Everlasting joy will be theirs."

Prayer Focus: Pray that the shame your child is carrying would be traded for a double portion of blessing and everlasting joy.

Philippians 1:6: "For I am confident of this very thing, that He who began a good work in you will perfect it until the day of Christ Jesus."

Prayer Focus: Remind God that He began a good work in your child when they were young, and claim His faithfulness to perfect it in His timing.

Hebrews 10:23: "Let us hold fast the confession of our hope without wavering, for He who promised is faithful."

Prayer Focus (for the Parent): Pray for your own ability to hold fast to hope, because you know the Promiser is faithful.

V. Praying for Your Own Strength and Peace (The Anchor)

These verses are for your daily survival, reminding you to seek comfort and strength from God.

Psalm 3:3: "But You, O Lord, are a shield about me, My glory, and the One who lifts my head."

Prayer Focus: Ask God to be your shield against shame and fear, and to lift your head when you feel defeated.

Isaiah 41:10: "Do not fear, for I am with you; Do not anxiously look about you, for I am your God. I will strengthen you, surely I will help you, Surely I will uphold you with My righteous right hand."

Prayer Focus: Claim the five promises: Do not fear, I am with you, I will strengthen you, I will help you, I will uphold you.

1 Peter 5:7: "casting all your anxiety on Him, because He cares for you."

Prayer Focus: Hurl the burden of your current anxiety about your child onto God because He cares for you personally.

Psalm 46:10: "Cease striving and know that I am God; I will be exalted among the nations, I will be exalted in the earth."

Prayer Focus: Pray for the grace to "cease striving" (stop trying to fix it) and rest in the knowledge of God's sovereignty.

Lamentations 3:25-26: "The Lord is good to those who wait for Him, To the person who seeks Him. It is good that he waits silently For the salvation of the Lord."

Prayer Focus: Pray for the ability to wait silently and expectantly for God's specific salvation (rescue) for your child.

Philippians 4:13: "I can do all things through Him who strengthens me."

Prayer Focus: Pray that God would strengthen you to love unconditionally, set boundaries firmly, and endure patiently.

Psalm 56:8: "You have taken account of my wanderings; Put my tears in Your bottle. Are they not in Your book?"

Prayer Focus: Acknowledge your deep grief and thank God that He has collected every one of your tears—they are not wasted.

Romans 5:5: "and hope does not disappoint, because the love of God has been poured out within our hearts through the Holy Spirit who was given to us."

Prayer Focus: Pray that the love of God would be poured into your heart, assuring you that the hope you have will not disappoint.

VI. Additional Powerful Promises (The Final Anchors)

Matthew 18:14: "So it is not the will of your Father who is in heaven that one of these little ones perish."

Prayer Focus: Remind God that it is not His will for your child to perish, and claim His redemptive will.

John 10:28: "and I give eternal life to them, and they will never perish; and no one will snatch them out of My hand."

Prayer Focus (for the future): Pray for the day your child is secure in Christ's hand, where no one (not the devil, not the world, not their own will) can snatch them away.

Isaiah 54:13: "And all your sons will be taught of the Lord; And the well-being of your sons will be great."

Prayer Focus: Claim the promise that your child will be taught by the Lord and their well-being will be great.

Psalm 37:4: "Delight yourself in the Lord; And He will give you the desires of your heart."

Prayer Focus: Pray for your child to find their delight in the Lord instead of worldly pleasures.

Jeremiah 31:3: "The Lord appeared to him from afar, saying, 'I have loved you with an everlasting love; Therefore I have drawn you with lovingkindness.'"

Prayer Focus: Pray for God's everlasting love to reach your child even from afar, drawing them with kindness and mercy.

1 Corinthians 10:13: "No temptation has overtaken you but such as is common to man; and faithful is God, who will not allow you to be tempted beyond what you are able, but with the temptation will provide the way of escape also, so that you will be able to endure it."

Prayer Focus: Pray that God will provide a way of escape from the specific temptations (addiction, lifestyle) your child faces.

Psalm 142:5: "I cried out to You, O Lord; I said, 'You are my refuge, My portion in the land of the living.'"

Prayer Focus (for the Parent): Claim God as your refuge and your portion, the only thing you truly need to sustain you.

Ephesians 3:20: "Now to Him who is able to do far more abundantly beyond all that we ask or think, according to the power that works within us,"

Prayer Focus: Ask God to work in your child's life far more abundantly than you can even imagine or conceive.

Matthew 7:11: "If you then, being evil, know how to give good gifts to your children, how much more will your Father who is in heaven give what is good to those who ask Him!"

Prayer Focus: Remind yourself that if you, an imperfect parent, desire good for your child, how much more does your perfect Heavenly Father desire and plan good for them.

Galatians 6:9: "Let us not lose heart in doing good, for in due time we will reap if we do not grow weary."

Prayer Focus: Pray for endurance and the spiritual strength to not grow weary, knowing that a harvest of joy and redemption will come in due time.

Use these scriptures as your constant spiritual ammunition. Your prayers are never wasted, and God's Word never returns void.

Paul Beersdorf

Tough Prayers

I will also encourage you to learn to pray tough prayers!

What are tough prayers? They are prayers we never thought we would have to pray over our children!

Here is an example:

"Dear God, I pray for my prodigal child this morning and bring them before your throne of mercy and grace. I pray that You will BREAK their plans today and that they would not have any success in those areas of their life that are keeping them from You and from us. Bring them to that low point in their life when all they can do is turn to You! We know that rock bottom can be a firm foundation!

I pray that they may have that sudden awakening moment and come to their senses.

Do whatever You need to do to break the strongholds and barriers in their life.

Drive away anyone who is a negative influence and impact on their life.

May they have no success in any relationship that does not honor You.

I pray for their restoration, their salvation, and I pray you will bring people of positive influence into their life and open their ears that they might hear. I pray all of this in the precious name of Jesus. Amen"

I never thought I would ever have to pray a prayer like that over my child and yet this is a daily prayer and petition that I bring before God every day. Along with lots of other prayers!!!

The next chapter will provide you with some guided scripture prayers about the character of God that we have learned over the years.

Good Company

It is one of the hardest things a parent can go through.

You raised them, you loved them, and you pointed them toward God—but now, they've walked away. You might feel like you're the only one staring at an empty chair or waiting for a phone call that never comes.

But here is the truth: You are in good company.

The Bible is full of "good parents" whose children took a wrong turn. Even God, the perfect Father, dealt with the first wayward children in a perfect garden.

Let's look at some of these families to see that you aren't alone and that a child's choice doesn't always mean the parents failed.

The Heartbreak of the First Family

Parents: Adam and Eve | Child: Cain

Imagine being the very first parents.

Adam and Eve lived in a perfect world and walked with God. They knew Him personally!

Yet, their firstborn son, Cain, allowed jealousy to take root in his heart. Even after God personally warned him to do the right thing, Cain chose a path of violence.

"Then the Lord said to Cain, 'Why are you angry? And why has your face fallen? If you do well, will not your face be cheerful? And if you do not do well, sin is lurking at the door; and its desire is for you, but you must master it.'" — **Genesis 4:6-7 (NASB)**

Cain didn't listen. He chose to walk away from his family and his Creator. If the first parents ever felt like they failed, they surely felt it then. But Cain's choice was his own.

When "Church Kids" Go Wayward

Parent: Samuel | Children: Joel and Abijah

Samuel was one of the greatest prophets in history.

He was a man of total integrity who listened to God from the time he was a little boy. You would think his kids would be just like him. But as they grew up, they chose a different path.

"His sons, however, did not walk in his ways, but turned aside after dishonest gain and took bribes and perverted justice." — **1 Samuel 8:3 (NASB)**

It's a heavy burden when a parent is serving God faithfully, yet their children don't "walk in their ways." Samuel's story reminds us that even when a parent is a spiritual giant, children still have the free will to make their own mistakes.

The High Cost of Rebellion

Parent: King David | Child: Absalom

David was called a "man after God's own heart."

He wrote the Psalms and loved the Lord deeply. But his son Absalom was the ultimate rebel. He didn't just leave home; he actively fought against his father's values and tried to take his kingdom.

Despite the rebellion and the public embarrassment, David's heart stayed soft toward his son. When war broke out, David gave these famous orders:

"The king charged Joab and Abishai and Ittai, saying, 'Deal gently for my sake with the young man Absalom.' And all the people heard when the king charged all the commanders concerning Absalom." — **2 Samuel 18:5 (NASB)**

David's story shows the "messy" side of grace. Even when a child is actively working against everything you stand for, a parent's heart still cries out for mercy.

The Famous Long Way Home

The Father in Jesus' Parable | Child: The Prodigal Son

Jesus told a story specifically for parents like you.

A son demanded his inheritance early — basically telling his father, "I wish you were dead" — and wasted everything in a far-off country.

The father didn't chase him down or force him to come home.

He waited.

He watched the horizon.

And when the son finally hit rock bottom, he remembered his father's goodness.

"But when he came to his senses, he said, 'How many of my father's hired men have more than enough bread, but I am dying here with hunger! I will get up and go to my father, and I will say to him, "Father, I have sinned against heaven, and in your sight; I am no longer worthy to be called your son; make me as one of your hired men."'" — **Luke 15:17-19 (NASB)**

The beautiful part of this story is that the father was already looking for him. The son "came to his senses," but the father's love had never changed.

Finding Peace in the Waiting

As you read these stories, notice a pattern:

1. **Choice:** Each child made their own choice, regardless of how "good" the parent was.

2. **Consequences:** Those choices led to pain, but often that pain was what eventually turned their hearts back.

3. **God's Presence:** God was present in every one of these stories, even when the parents were grieving.

Your child's story isn't over yet. Just like the father of the prodigal son, you can keep the light on and the door open, trusting that God is the Great Seeker of lost sheep.

A Prayer for the Waiting Parent

Sometimes, the weight of waiting is just too heavy.

You've talked to your child, you've talked to your friends, and you've talked to yourself—but the most important person to talk to is the Father who loves your child even more than you do.

God tells us that we don't have to carry this worry alone. He invites us to trade our "what-ifs" for His peace.

"Be anxious for nothing, but in everything by prayer and supplication with thanksgiving let your requests be made known to God. And the peace of God, which surpasses all comprehension, will guard your hearts and your minds in Christ Jesus." — Philippians 4:6-7 (NASB)

If you don't know what to say today, you can use this prayer as a starting point:

Dear Lord - I come to You today with a heavy heart. You know my child's name, and You know exactly where they are—not just where they are living, but where their heart is. Lord, I admit that I am tired of worrying. I'm tired of trying to fix things that only You can fix.

Right now, I place my child back into Your hands. I ask that You would protect them and bring people into their lives who will point them back to You.

Please help them "come to their senses," just like the prodigal son did in the pigpen.

Help them remember the love they were raised with.

And Lord, please take care of me, too. Give me Your peace that doesn't make sense to the world. Help me to sleep tonight knowing that You never sleep and that You are watching over my family. Help me to be ready to run to them with open arms whenever they decide to come home.

In Jesus' name, Amen.

Sources and References

- *New American Standard Bible (NASB)*, Copyright © 1960, 1962, 1963, 1968, 1971, 1972, 1973, 1975, 1977, 1995 by The Lockman Foundation.

- *The Holy Bible,* Genesis 4:6-7, 1 Samuel 8:3, 2 Samuel 18:5, Luke 15:17-19.

- Commentary on the Life of Samuel, *Holman Bible Handbook*.

- Life Application Study Bible, *Notes on the Parable of the Lost Son*.

Paul Beersdorf

Famous Prodigals

If you think you are alone in the journey, here are four famous prodigals who all returned to the faith! Never give up hope!

1. Saint Augustine of Hippo

Saint Augustine of Hippo spent the longest time as a prodigal among these figures, wandering for approximately **fifteen years** (from his late teens until his conversion at age 31 in 386 AD). His journey was one of intellectual and moral rebellion, characterized by rejecting his Christian upbringing, pursuing a hedonistic lifestyle, taking a mistress, and actively seeking truth in heretical philosophical movements like Manichaeism. He resisted the relentless prayers of his mother, Monica, until his famous conversion in a garden in Milan. Augustine's story is a powerful testimony to enduring maternal prayer and God's power to reach the most brilliant and determined intellectual rebels.

Source/Citation: Augustine. *Confessions.* (Translated by R.S. Pine-Coffin or Henry Chadwick).

2. John Newton

John Newton's period as a prodigal lasted approximately **fifteen years** (from his late teens until his full conversion around 1754). His path was marked by extreme moral degradation and a defiance that shocked even his rough sailing companions. He abandoned his faith, became involved in the brutal African slave trade, and lived a life he later described as utterly profane and rebellious. His initial "awakening" began during a terrifying storm at sea in 1748, but his full conversion took several more years of wrestling. His deep repentance led him to abandon the slave trade, become an Anglican minister, and write the enduring hymn of redemption, "Amazing Grace."

Source/Citation: *An Authentic Narrative of Some Remarkable and Interesting Particulars in the Life of ******** Communicated in a Series of Letters to the Reverend Mr. Haweis.* (The John Newton Project).

3. Franklin Graham

Franklin Graham experienced his prodigal years for approximately **six to seven years** (from age 16 until his conversion in 1974 at age 22). As the son of Billy Graham, his rebellion was highly visible and characterized by rejecting his parents' religious world. He was involved in heavy drinking, confrontation with the police, and a rebellious lifestyle that caused intense concern for his family. His turning point came during a challenging trip to the Alaskan wilderness, where he made a personal commitment to Christ, ending his tumultuous separation. His journey is often cited as a modern example that piety and fame do not inoculate children from the temptation to stray.

Source/Citation: Graham, Franklin. *Rebel with a Cause: A Story of a Prodigal Son.* Thomas Nelson, 1995.

4. Louis Zamperini

Louis Zamperini's period of being a prodigal was relatively short, lasting approximately **four years** (from his return in 1945 to his conversion in 1949). Zamperini was a decorated Olympic runner and WWII hero who survived horrific torture as a Japanese Prisoner of War. However, his trauma manifested as severe Post-Traumatic Stress Disorder (PTSD) and an addiction to alcohol, which nearly destroyed his marriage and alienated him from his family. His return to faith and subsequent healing occurred suddenly when his wife convinced him to attend a Billy Graham crusade in Los Angeles. His story demonstrates that the "riotous living" of a prodigal can be self-destructive, trauma-fueled isolation, not just financial waste.

Source/Citation: Hillenbrand, Laura. *Unbroken: A World War II Story of Survival, Resilience, and Redemption.* Random House, 2010.

Characteristics of God

It was during a season of testing and trials that I struggled with how to praise God. There were days when I did not want to be thankful or grateful and life was tough. The days were long and the nights were longer.

However, in those tough times, I choose to lean into God and the Bible and look for ways to praise God no matter the circumstances. I turned to the Psalms and started looking for the characteristics of God that I could be thankful for – no matter my situation or challenge.

It was through this time of study and reflection that I compiled this list and have since made it part of my daily prayer routine.

I liked to follow the ACTS form of prayer:

A = Adoration
C = Confession
T = Thanksgiving
S = Supplication

What I did was add this list of characteristics of God to my thankful list and praise Him each day for being all these things in my life! While I may change and vacillate, God does not change.

It has helped transform the way I view God each day and provided me with a much more positive attitude and outlook. It is with a grateful and thankful heart that I start each day.

I know this list is not fully comprehensive of all the characteristics of God. It is only a list compiled from the Psalms. Since David wrote the majority of the Psalms and was a man after God's own heart, I feel like this is a good starting place to better understand and praise God.

My goal is to be able to praise God no matter what! A tall order indeed!!

While I know I will fail some days, it is in the striving towards this goal that will help me achieve a closer walk with God.

My hope and prayer is that this devotional will draw you closer to God and help you to praise and worship Him more no matter your circumstances.

Blessing to you! I hope you enjoy this devotional.

These are the different Characteristics of God from Psalms:

Rock	Hope	Provider
Refuge	Help	Protector
Rescuer	Healer	Provision
Redeemer	Hiding place	Peace
Reviver		Portion
Reliever	Fortress	
Refiner		Vindicator
Shepard	Deliverer	Avenger
Salvation	Defender	
Sustainer	Defense	Keeper
Support		
Strength	Comforter	Light
Stronghold	Confidence	
Shield	Contender	Guide
Song		
Shade		Trust

1. **Rock**
    - **Psalm 18:2** - *The Lord is my rock and my fortress and my deliverer, My God, my rock, in whom I take refuge; My shield and the horn of my salvation, my stronghold.*

2. **Refuge**
    - **Psalm 46:1** - *God is our refuge and strength, A very present help in trouble.*

3. **Rescuer**
    - **Psalm 18:48** - *He delivers me from my enemies; Surely You lift me above those who rise up against me; You rescue me from the violent man.*

4. **Redeemer**
    - **Psalm 78:35** - *And they remembered that God was their rock, And the Most High God their Redeemer.*

5. **Reviver**
    - **Psalm 119:40** - *Behold, I long for Your precepts; Revive me through Your righteousness.*

6. **Reliever**
    - **Psalm 4:1** - *Answer me when I call, O God of my righteousness! You have relieved me in my distress; Be gracious to me and hear my prayer.*

7. **Refiner**
    - **Psalm 66:10** - *For You have tried us, O God; You have refined us as silver is refined.*

8. **Hope**
    - **Psalm 71:5** - *For You are my hope, O Lord God; You are my confidence since my youth.*

9. **Help**

    o **Psalm 121:2** - *My help comes from the Lord, Who made heaven and earth.*

10. **Healer**

    o **Psalm 30:2** - *O Lord my God, I cried to You for help, And You healed me.*

11. **Hiding place**

    o **Psalm 119:114** - *You are my hiding place and my shield; I wait for Your word.*

12. **Provider**

    o **Psalm 23:1** - *The Lord is my shepherd, I shall not want.*

13. **Protector**

    o **Psalm 121:7** - *The Lord will protect you from all evil; He will keep your soul.*

14. **Provision**

    o **Psalm 68:10** - *Your creatures settled in it; You provided in Your goodness for the poor, O God.*

15. **Peace**

    o **Psalm 29:11** - *The Lord will give strength to His people; The Lord will bless His people with peace.*

16. **Portion**

    o **Psalm 73:26** - *My flesh and my heart may fail, But God is the rock of my heart and my portion forever.*

17. **Shepherd**

    o **Psalm 23:1** - *The Lord is my shepherd, I shall not want.*

18. **Salvation**
    - **Psalm 68:19** - *Blessed be the Lord, who daily bears our burden, The God who is our salvation. Selah.*

19. **Sustainer**
    - **Psalm 145:14** - *The Lord sustains all who fall And raises up all who are bowed down.*

20. **Support**
    - **Psalm 18:18** - *They confronted me in the day of my disaster, But the Lord was my support.*

21. **Strength**
    - **Psalm 28:7** - *The Lord is my strength and my shield; My heart trusts in Him, and I am helped; Therefore my heart triumphs, And with my song I shall thank Him.*

22. **Stronghold**
    - **Psalm 37:39** - *But the salvation of the righteous is from the Lord; He is their stronghold in time of trouble.*

23. **Shield**
    - **Psalm 3:3** - *But You, O Lord, are a shield about me, My glory, and the One who lifts my head.*

24. **Song**
    - **Psalm 118:14** – *The Lord is my strength and song. And he has become by salvation*

25. **Shade**
    - **Psalm 121:5** - *The Lord is your keeper; The Lord is your shade on your right hand.*

26. **Fortress**
    - **Psalm 91:2** - *I will say to the Lord, "My refuge and my fortress, My God, in whom I trust!"*

27. **Deliverer**

    o **Psalm 70:5** - *But I am afflicted and needy; Hurry to me, O God! You are my help and my deliverer; O Lord, do not delay.*

28. **Defender**

    o **Psalm 91:4** - *He will cover you with His pinions, And under His wings you may seek refuge; His faithfulness is a shield and bulwark.*

29. **Defense**

    o **Psalm 27:1** - *The Lord is my light and my salvation; Whom shall I fear? The Lord is the defense of my life; Whom shall I dread?*

30. **Comforter**

    o **Psalm 23:4** - *Even though I walk through the valley of the shadow of death, I fear no evil, for You are with me; Your rod and Your staff, they comfort me.*

31. **Confidence**

    o **Psalm 71:5** - *For You are my hope, O Lord God; You are my confidence since my youth.*

32. **Contender**

    o **Psalm 35:1** - *Contend, O Lord, with those who contend with me; Fight against those who fight against me.*

33. **Vindicator**

    o **Psalm 7:8** - *The Lord judges the peoples; Vindicate me, O Lord, according to my righteousness and my integrity that is in me.*

34. **Avenger**

    o **Psalm 94:1** - *O Lord, God of vengeance, O God of vengeance, shine forth!*

35. **Keeper**

    - **Psalm 121:5** - *The Lord is your keeper; The Lord is your shade on your right hand.*

36. **Light**

    - **Psalm 27:1** - *The Lord is my light and my salvation; Whom shall I fear? The Lord is the defense of my life; Whom shall I dread?*

37. **Guide**

    - **Psalm 73:24** - *With Your counsel You will guide me, And afterward receive me to glory.*

38. **Trust**

    - **Psalm 9:10** - *And those who know Your name will put their trust in You, For You, O Lord, have not forsaken those who seek You.*

    - **Psalm 56:11** - *In God I have put my trust, I shall not be afraid. What can man do to me?*

Day 1

The Loss

The Unmet Expectation: Acknowledging the Loss

When your adult child walks away from the faith, the family, or a healthy life path, you enter a uniquely painful season known as ambiguous loss.

Your child is still physically present, or at least still alive, but the relationship you had—and the future you had meticulously planned—is gone. It is the grief of a living person. This is the unmet expectation—the sudden, brutal realization that the beautiful dream you carried for your family has shattered.

It is absolutely vital for your healing to acknowledge and name this loss. You are not just mourning a difficult situation; you are mourning the death of a hope, a dream, and a lifetime of investment. Until you admit the pain is real and deep, you will be unable to receive the comfort God offers.

The Double Grief of the Christian Parent

Parents in this situation go through a double grief, and it's important to give yourself full permission to feel both parts of it without guilt or shame:

1. The Loss of the Present Person

You miss the phone calls, the shared laughter, the meaningful spiritual conversations, the regular holidays, and the comfort of knowing your child is safe and well.

The physical or emotional distance creates a hollow ache in your daily life that can mimic the physical symptoms of mourning. You miss who they were or, more acutely, who they should be in the life of the family.

2. The Loss of the Future Dream (The Spiritual Ache)

This is often the hardest and deepest part of the wound for a believer.

You grieve the grandchildren who might never know Jesus, the wedding that may never happen, the family unity that will never be photographed, and the assurance that your child is safe in Christ for eternity. This is the ultimate unmet expectation—the failure of the generational faith transfer that you prayed for, taught toward, and sacrificed for your entire life.

The weight of this double grief can bring enormous emotional and physical pain. You may feel actual illness, exhaustion, or chronic anxiety. This is not a sign of weak faith; it is the natural response of a loving heart that has been broken. You can't heal what you refuse to acknowledge. You must allow yourself to mourn the death of the dream.

The Tyranny of Shame and Silence

One of the most destructive forces in this journey is shame. We worry that if we speak openly about our child's choices, people will judge us. The inner voice says: You must have failed. You didn't pray hard enough. Your witness must not have been authentic.

This shame is a lie from the enemy used to keep you isolated and silent. When you hide, you cut yourself off from the comfort of the Holy Spirit and the support of the community God intended for your healing.

The Bible makes it clear that there is a time for all things, including an honest time to mourn and weep:

"There is an appointed time for everything. And there is a time for every event under heaven—... A time to weep and a time to laugh; a time to mourn and a time to dance" (Ecclesiastes 3:1, 4, NASB).

You are currently in a time to weep and mourn. That is okay. Allow yourself to feel it. Name the sadness and the shame you feel, and then bring both directly to God, whose grace is sufficient for your failures (real or perceived).

Letting the Wave Push You to the Rock

The great Baptist preacher Charles Spurgeon faced severe depression and physical illness throughout his ministry, and he knew the reality of overwhelming trials. He understood that faith does not magically cancel sorrow; it simply gives it a safe place to land.

Spurgeon is often quoted as saying, "I have learned to kiss the wave that throws me against the Rock of Ages."

Think about that image. When a wave crashes over you, your natural instinct is to fight it, to flail and gasp for air. That fighting only drains your strength. To kiss the wave means to accept the painful trial (the wave) because you realize its true purpose: it is pushing you with unexpected force directly toward Christ (the Rock of Ages).

Your grief over your child is the powerful wave. Acknowledge it, surrender to it, and allow its force to push you into a closer, firmer grip on Jesus than you've ever had before.

A Command for Casting the Burden

When you name your grief and shame, you are taking it out of the hidden, dark place of isolation and bringing it into the light of God's sovereign grace. This is where active healing begins.

We are commanded to be humble and to transfer our anxiety to God because He cares for us. This is an active step:

"Therefore humble yourselves under the mighty hand of God, that He may exalt you at the proper time, casting all your anxiety on Him, because He cares for you" (1 Peter 5:6–7, NASB).

The Greek word used for "casting" in this verse means to literally "hurl" or "throw off" the weight with great force. It's an action of transfer. You are not meant to carry this crippling burden.

Your Action Step: When you feel the double grief—the loss of the present child and the loss of the future dream—stop and consciously hurl that specific anxiety onto God. Remind yourself that you are throwing it onto a Father who is mighty enough to hold it and whose care for you is the motivation for the entire command.

Acknowledge your loss. Release the shame. And let God carry the immense weight of the shattered dream. This foundational step of honest grief will prepare you for the difficult work of faith that lies ahead.

References

- Ecclesiastes 3:1, 4 (NASB)
- 1 Peter 5:6-7 (NASB)

Historical and Anecdotal References:

Charles Spurgeon Quote: "I have learned to kiss the wave..." This reflects his personal struggle with sorrow and his reliance on God's sovereignty.

- *Source: Commonly attributed to Charles Spurgeon, reflecting the theme of trials driving believers to Christ.*

Reflection

Take a few minutes to reflect and meditate on what you just read. Write down your thoughts and take time to pray and praise God.

_____
_____
_____
_____
_____
_____
_____
_____
_____
_____
_____
_____
_____
_____
_____
_____
_____
_____
_____

Day 2

Be Still

"Be still, and know that I am God; I will be exalted among the nations, I will be exalted in the earth" (Psalm 46:10, NASB).

Listening for the Whisper in the Wilderness

If you're reading this, you probably know what it feels like to live with a dull, constant ache in your heart or mind.

It's the kind of pain that doesn't just come and go—it settles in, sometimes in your chest, sometimes in your throat, sometimes in the back of your mind. It's the unique and terrible grief of loving an adult child who has chosen a path away from your family, your values, and maybe most painfully, the faith you once shared together.

In this kind of wilderness season, the world's noise doesn't sound like distractions anymore. It sounds like accusations: "You should have done more." "You failed them somehow."

It sounds like worry: "Are they safe?" "Will they ever come back?"

And it sounds like despair: "Does God even hear my prayers anymore?"

The noise of our personal grief can be so loud that it drowns out the very voice we need to hear most: the reassuring, steady voice of our heavenly Father.

This chapter isn't about fixing your child (nor will you find that anywhere in this book). It's about learning to unplug from the static of fear and doubt so you can tune in to God's strength, which is the only thing that will sustain you through this journey (whether it is a long or short journey).

Paul Beersdorf

The Static of Sorrow

When a child walks away, a parent's life becomes dominated by internal static. We are constantly monitoring, analyzing, and replaying events. We spend so much energy on the "what-ifs" and the "if-onlys." That mental and emotional noise is a massive barrier to hearing God. I have been stuck here before, and urge you to move quickly through these "what-ifs" and "if-onlys". This in unproductive time!

In fact, sometimes we can even treat God like another source of noise — we approach Him with a long, urgent list of demands, hoping He'll shout the solutions we want. But the Bible reminds us that in times of deep turmoil, we are commanded to slow down and listen for Him differently.

The Psalmist writes, *"Be still, and know that I am God; I will be exalted among the nations, I will be exalted in the earth" (Psalm 46:10, NASB).*

For a parent carrying this heavy burden, "Be still" feels impossible. It feels like asking a boat that is being tossed in a storm to just stop moving. But remember, the command is not to stop caring; it's to stop striving and worrying.

It's about consciously moving your focus from the massive, churning problem (your child's situation) to the massive, unchanging person of (God).

When we try to force an outcome or control a child's choices (which almost always leads to failure), we are shouting out our own will.

When we are still, we allow the divine truth to finally settle: that God's plan is bigger than our pain, and His love for our child is greater than even our own overwhelming love.

Finding God in the Gentle Blowing

Think about the story of the prophet Elijah in the Old Testament. Elijah was facing a crisis of faith and fear. He felt isolated and defeated after performing an incredible miracle (he had defeated all the prophets of Baal), and he ran to a cave because he was being pursued by the wicked queen Jezebel who wanted to kill him..

He was expecting God to show up in a massive, dramatic way—a way that matched the drama of his own emotional storm.

When God showed up on the mountain, this is what happened: "So He said, 'Go out and stand on the mountain before the Lord.' And behold, the Lord was passing by! And a great and strong wind was tearing the mountains and breaking the rocks in pieces before the Lord; but the Lord was not in the wind. And after the wind an earthquake, but the Lord was not in the earthquake. And after the earthquake a fire, but the Lord was not in the fire; and after the fire a sound of a gentle blowing" (1 Kings 19:11-12, NASB).

This is such a crucial lesson for parents in the wilderness:

The Wind represents the loud chaos of the world—the negative messages your child is consuming, the culture pushing against faith, the judgmental voices of others. God is often not in that chaos.

The Earthquake represents the emotional devastation—the gut-wrenching pain, the panic, the collapse of your hopes. God is often not in the raw, immediate devastation.

The Fire represents the cleansing and fierce judgment you might want to call down—the desire for God to step in and force a sudden, painful change. God is often not in the severity you might demand.

Instead, God was in the "sound of a gentle blowing" (sometimes translated as a still, small voice).

When your heart is breaking, you must stop listening for the wind, the earthquake, or the fire (even though you might think that will be justice and satisfaction).

You must learn to listen for the whisper of assurance that reminds you of God's unchanging character and His promises.

As the great Christian writer and poet C.S. Lewis once observed about God's presence, "We are far too easily pleased." In our parenting struggles, we are often too easily pleased with loud, dramatic answers, when what we truly need is the quiet, sustained comfort of His presence.

Practical Steps to Unplug and Tune In

Tuning into God isn't passive; it's a deliberate act of spiritual discipline. When your heart is consumed by worry over your adult child, here are practical ways to create space for God's whisper.

1. Stop Chasing the Noise of the Situation

When you feel the urge to obsessively search your child's social media, or talk endlessly about the situation with friends, or engage in mental replays of the past, stop. That is chasing the noise.

Instead, follow the instruction given by the Apostle Paul: "Do not be anxious about anything, but in everything by prayer and pleading with thanksgiving let your requests be made known to God. And the peace of God, which surpasses all comprehension, will guard your hearts and minds in Christ Jesus" (Philippians 4:6-7, NASB).

When the anxiety hits, immediately turn it into a prayer. Don't just ask God to fix your child; thank God that He is sovereign, and that He knows where your child is, and that His timing is perfect. This deliberate act of thanksgiving is the 'off switch' for anxiety.

2. Guard Your Gaze

It is easy to let the weight of your child's choices become your only focus, and cause it to obscure your vision of God. The writer of Hebrews gives us this powerful reminder:

"Let us run with endurance the race that is set before us, fixing our eyes on Jesus, the author and perfecter of faith, who for the joy set before Him endured the cross, despising the shame, and has sat down at the right hand of the throne of God" (Hebrews 12:1-2, NASB).

When your eyes are fixed on Jesus, you are reminded that your salvation and your peace do not depend on your child's decisions. Your race — your life of faith — is separate from theirs. Your primary responsibility is to finish your race well.

3. Embrace the Inner Room

Jesus taught us the importance of private, focused prayer: "But when you pray, go into your inner room, close your door, and pray to your Father who is in secret; and your Father who sees what is done in secret will reward you" (Matthew 6:6, NASB).

Your "inner room" is where you go to be absolutely alone with God, free from interruption. For a grieving parent, this needs to be a daily refuge. Go there, not to tell God what He should do, but to simply sit in His presence. It's in this quiet, secret space that God will refill the emotional well that your painful situation constantly drains.

Turning to stillness and unplugging will look different to everyone. For me it is about going for a quiet walk (usually in the woods or on a quiet trail). You may find your stillness on the back deck, or in a spare room or even in your vehicle. The key is finding some place quiet.

The famous evangelist Billy Graham understood the profound importance of spending time alone with God. He said, "We are the Bibles the world is reading; we are the creeds the world is needing; we are the sermons the world is heeding."

For us, this means the way we handle the quiet pain and trust God in our waiting speaks a much louder sermon than any lecture we could give our child.

Ultimately, your hope is not found in the sudden return or conversion of your child, but in the unwavering love and faithfulness of God. When you unplug the noise of worry and tune into His quiet peace, you can become a source of rest, stability, and quiet hope for those around you, no matter how long the wilderness season lasts.

References

- 1 Kings 19:11-12 (NASB)
- Psalm 46:10 (NASB)
- Philippians 4:6-7 (NASB)
- Hebrews 12:1-2 (NASB)
- Matthew 6:6 (NASB)

Historical and Anecdotal References:

C.S. Lewis Quote: "We are far too easily pleased," from The Weight of Glory.

- Reference: *https://www.cslewis.com/*

Billy Graham Quote: A widely attributed quote emphasizing Christian conduct.

- Reference: *https://billygraham.org/*

Reflection

Take a few minutes to reflect and meditate on what you just read. Write down your thoughts and take time to pray and praise God.

_____
_____
_____
_____
_____
_____
_____
_____
_____
_____
_____
_____
_____
_____
_____
_____
−

Day 3
Don't Give Up

Don't Give Up: The Power of Enduring Hope

If you are a parent whose adult child has walked away from home, family, or faith, you know what it means to be truly exhausted. It's not just physical exhaustion from lack of sleep; it's soul exhaustion. It's deep and overwhelming exhaustion!

The road you are on may be a long one (I hope and pray it will be short), and often, the heaviest burden is the constant temptation to simply give up on hope. You might feel like your prayers are bouncing off the ceiling, like your love isn't enough, and like the separation will last forever.

The world—and sometimes your own mind—will tell you it's time to move on, to accept defeat, or to put the pain aside. But as followers of Jesus, we have a different call. Our hope is not based on what we see today; it is anchored in the promise of a God who never gives up on us, and who calls us to endure.

This chapter is a reminder that your spiritual strength is not measured by the speed of the answer, but by the steadiness of your hope. You are not just hanging on; you are holding fast to a powerful promise.

The Great Endurance Race

Think of your current situation as a marathon (26.2 miles). Not a quick sprint, but a long, grueling endurance race. In a marathon, the most dangerous part isn't the beginning when you're full of adrenaline and excitement, or the end when the finish line is in sight. It's the middle miles—the point where you are completely spent, you feel utterly alone, and you can't see the end yet and the beginning seems like a life time ago. That is when you want to quit.

The Bible has a lot to say about enduring these middle miles of life. In fact, one of the most powerful passages written to Christians who were facing severe trials, including the loss of loved ones, reminds us of the finish line:

"Let us run with endurance the race that is set before us, fixing our eyes on Jesus, the author and perfecter of faith, who for the joy set before Him endured the cross, despising the shame, and has sat down at the right hand of the throne of God" (Hebrews 12:1-2, NASB).

Notice the language here: "run with endurance." Endurance isn't sprinting; it's consistent forward motion, even when every muscle aches. For parents praying for a wayward child, endurance means:

Consistent Prayer: Praying not just when you feel hopeful, but especially when you feel despair. Pray without ceasing!

Consistent Love: Always keeping your heart open to your child, even when their actions make it difficult.

Consistent Faith: Refusing to let your current reality redefine God's character.

You are not running this race alone, and you are not running toward a question mark. You are running with your eyes fixed on Jesus, who endured the ultimate separation and pain (the cross) for the joy of bringing us home. If He endured the worst for us, He can certainly give us the strength to endure our painful watching and waiting.

A Historical Look at Sticking With It

The idea of not giving up, even when things look impossible, is a theme that runs through human history and achievement. It often takes far longer for a big breakthrough than we ever expect.

Consider the inventor Thomas Edison. When he was trying to create a functional electric light bulb, he didn't just try a few different materials. It is famously claimed that he tried thousands of different combinations and filaments before finding one that would work reliably. When a reporter asked him how he felt about failing so many times, his response was powerful and famous:

"I have not failed. I've just found 10,000 ways that won't work."

Edison didn't give up because he reframed the "failures." They weren't reasons to quit; they were necessary steps on the path to the solution.

As a Christian parent, you can apply this perspective to your prayers. When you pray for your child and nothing seems to change immediately, you haven't failed. You have simply participated in a prayer that may be one of many necessary steps in God's long, slow work on your child's heart, which is a process only He can fully see and control.

The Power of Persistent Prayer

There is a powerful and challenging story Jesus tells that speaks directly to the parent who feels exhausted from asking: the parable of the persistent widow.

In this story (found in Luke 18:1-8), a poor widow keeps going to an unjust judge to ask for help. The judge doesn't care about her, but she keeps bothering him until finally, he gives in, saying, "Even though I do not fear God nor regard man, yet because this widow bothers me, I will give her legal protection, otherwise by continually coming she will wear me out" (Luke 18:4-5, NASB).

Jesus didn't just tell this story to show that God is like a mean and grumpy, unjust judge—He tells us this story to show the contrast. If a heartless judge eventually gives in to persistence, how much more will the loving, just, and good Father respond to the faithful, persistent prayers of His children?

Jesus ends the story with a challenge: "Now, will not God bring about justice for His elect who cry to Him day and night, and will He delay long with them? I tell you that He will bring about justice for them quickly. However, when the Son of Man comes, will He find faith on the earth?" (Luke 18:7-8, NASB).

That final question is pointed directly at us: Will you find faith? Will you keep believing while you wait? Your job is not to give up. Your job is to keep crying out to Him day and night, trusting that God is working, even when you can't see the evidence.   Our timing may not be God's timing and our plans may not be God's plans.

The Gift of Waiting

When we pray for something as huge as the restoration of a child's soul, the waiting can feel like a punishment. But what if the waiting itself is a gift from God, designed to strengthen you?

The Apostle Paul, who endured incredible hardship, wrote about the unique blessings that come from waiting on God:

"And not only this, but we also celebrate in our tribulations, knowing that tribulation brings about perseverance; and perseverance, proven character; and proven character, hope; and hope does not disappoint, because the love of God has been poured out into our hearts through the Holy Spirit who was given to us" (Romans 5:3-5, NASB).

Right now, your trial (tribulation) is producing perseverance—your refusal to give up. And that perseverance is creating proven character—a deep, unshakable faith that has been tested and shown to be real. And this proven character is helping to solidify your hope, which will never let you down.

This means that while you are praying for your child, God is also using this time to deepen and strengthen your faith. This painful journey is forging something precious in your character that would never have been developed otherwise.

The renowned German philosopher Immanuel Kant once stated, "He who is unwilling to work, let him not eat." While this is a harsh statement about labor, the spiritual truth is similar: The most meaningful rewards often come only after the hard, consistent work of faith, prayer, and endurance.

Don't let your waiting be passive; let it be an active, persistent work of faith.

Your Assignment: The Steadfast Heart

So, what does "Don't Give Up" look like today?

It means that when you are tempted to stop praying, you pray a single, simple sentence instead: "Lord, I trust You."

It means that when you feel yourself closing your heart to your child out of self-protection, you remind yourself that your love for them is a reflection of God's perfect, unconditional love for both of you.

And it means holding onto the truth that God's love for your child is even more constant and enduring than your own. You can release the burden of their salvation back to Him, while you cling to the promise that the God who started a good work in you and in your family "will perform it until the day of Christ Jesus" (Philippians 1:6, NASB).

Don't give up. The One who promised is faithful, and your endurance is a powerful testament to His unwavering love.

References

- Hebrews 12:1-2 (NASB)
- Luke 18:4-5 (NASB)
- Luke 18:7-8 (NASB)
- Romans 5:3-5 (NASB)
- Philippians 1:6 (NASB)

Historical and Anecdotal References:

Thomas Edison Quote: "I have not failed. I've just found 10,000 ways that won't work." This famous quote is widely attributed to him regarding his efforts with the light bulb.

- *Reference: https://www.history.com/topics/inventions/thomas-edison*

Immanuel Kant Quote: "He who is unwilling to work, let him not eat." This concept is often cited in discussions of ethics and responsibility.

- *Reference: https://plato.stanford.edu/entries/kant/*

Paul Beersdorf

Reflection

Take a few minutes to reflect and meditate on what you just read. Write down your thoughts and take time to pray and praise God.

_____
_____
_____
_____
_____
_____
_____
_____
_____
_____
_____
_____
_____
_____
_____
_____
_____
_____
_____
_____

Day 4

Don't Give In

Holding the Line: Love Without Compromise

If you are a Christian parent of a wayward adult child, you have likely faced the moment of the impossible choice from your child saying or implying something like this: "If you really love me, you'll accept and affirm these choices I have made." Even though they know that it goes against everything you taught them and everything you have modeled and believed.

This is the moment of the squeeze. Your child is demanding that you sacrifice your core beliefs — your deeply held Christian values — as the price of being in a relationship with them. It feels like a painful, zero-sum game: either you compromise your faith to keep the peace, or you stand for truth and risk further separation.

The temptation to compromise is enormous. You might worry, "If I don't give in, I'll push them even further away. Maybe my silence is enough. Maybe I just have to swallow my convictions for the sake of reconciliation."

But as followers of Christ, we are called to hold to both love and truth. The truth is that Jesus never asks us to trade our integrity for comfort. This chapter is about setting and maintaining a biblical boundary — a fence of faith — that protects your soul without shutting the door on your child.

For a real life perspective, we have been faced with this very choice in almost those exact words above from our children. Our choice was to choose God, our faith and values first.

And as of the writing of this book, it has caused our children to become even more distant from us.

They have embraced the world and the lies from the world. It was not an easy conversation with them, but it has actually brought about peace in our life as we fully released them to God. They chose to cut us off, but we did not cut them off and we remain open and available to them.

The Biblical Foundation: Love and Truth

It is vital to understand that compromising your values is not a demonstration of Christ-like love; it is often an act of spiritual fear. True biblical love always walks hand-in-hand with truth.

We see this perfect balance in the person of Jesus. He was the most loving person who ever lived, and yet He never hesitated to speak hard truths. The Apostle John describes Him this way: "And the Word became flesh, and dwelt among us; and we saw His glory, glory as of the only Son from the Father, full of grace and truth" (John 1:14, NASB).

Jesus was full of grace (unconditional love, mercy, and kindness) and truth (God's unchanging standard and reality). We must strive for the same fullness.

When your adult child demands you affirm a choice that is contrary to God's Word, they are asking you to throw away the truth to give them grace. But grace without truth is meaningless; it's like a compliment that isn't earned. And truth without grace is harsh; it's like a judge with no mercy.

Your job as a Christian parent is to hold the two together:

Grace: Never stop loving them. Never stop welcoming them into your home (if safe). Never stop praying.

Truth: Never state, imply, or behave as if you agree with or approve of choices that the Bible clearly calls sin.

This means you are choosing to love them as a person, while holding firm to your convictions about their choices.

The Danger of the Slippery Slope

History gives us countless examples of how small compromises, made out of a desire for peace or approval, lead to massive spiritual downfalls.

Consider the example of Judas Maccabeus and the Jewish people during the Hellenistic period (around the second century B.C.). They were faced with the overwhelming cultural pressure from the powerful Greek Empire.

There were many Jewish leaders who were tempted to compromise their religious laws (like circumcision, Sabbath observance, and dietary rules) just to fit in and avoid persecution. Some of them even argued that these compromises were necessary to achieve "peace" with the dominant culture.

Judas Maccabeus and his followers refused to be vassals. They believed that even small compromises would lead to the total collapse of their faith and identity. They understood that where you draw the line today determines where you stand tomorrow and forever. Their refusal to yield, even when they were outnumbered and facing violence, helped to preserve the identity of Israel.

For us, the compromise is rarely about physical violence, but about emotional blackmail: "If you don't compromise your faith, I will cut you off." This feels like a threat to the life of the relationship. But you must remember that the moment you compromise your Christian identity, you lose the very foundation that makes you able to help them in the first place.

The great Baptist preacher Charles Spurgeon understood the spiritual danger of mixing truth with error. He said, "If there be but one point of the compass wrong, though a man should sail all the rest correctly, he will be sure to go astray."

When you compromise your values, you take your spiritual compass and intentionally turn it just one point wrong. You might think you can still steer the ship, but eventually, you will sail far off course (and very likely in to a rocky shore).

How to Build the Boundary

Holding the line is less about what you say to your child and more about what you do and don't do in your own life and home.

1. Define Your Sanctuary

Your home and your personal life are your sanctuaries. This means you do not allow your values to be violated within the physical space or customs of your family life.

For example, if a child demands that you host or celebrate an event that violates your biblical belief , you can say (with grace and love): "I love you and I love having you in my life. I cannot, however, host this particular type of event in my home because of my faith or I cannot attend a particular event because of my faith. But I would love to take you out to dinner the next night, just us, to spend time with you."

This is an act of holding the line: You do not compromise your home, but you do not stop loving your child.

2. Guard Your Tongue, Speak Your Identity

You do not need to constantly preach or argue. You simply need to live out your convictions clearly.

The key scripture here is found in Paul's letter to the Ephesians: "Therefore, laying aside falsehood, SPEAK TRUTH EACH ONE OF YOU WITH HIS NEIGHBOR, for we are members of one another" (Ephesians 4:25, NASB).

When confronted, you don't have to win an argument. You just have to speak your truth simply and consistently, showing that your convictions are a part of your very identity, not a weapon you use against them.

Example: When asked, "Do you accept my choice?" a loving, non-compromising answer is, "I love you completely and you are welcome here. However, my faith and the Bible teaches me that this particular choice is not God's best, and that is where I have to stand. That won't change my love for you."

(In our family our saying has always been " **I love you no matter what**" ILYNMW – my prodigal son actually has this as a tattoo on his arm).

3. Take Your Pain to the Father, Not to the Public

The immense pressure to compromise often comes from the loneliness and shame we feel as parents. When the pain is overwhelming, go immediately to your "inner room" for strength.

Jesus taught the importance of this private sanctuary: "But when you pray, go into your inner room, close your door, and pray to your Father who is in secret; and your Father who sees what is done in secret will reward you" (Matthew 6:6, NASB).

The strength to say no to compromise in public comes from the strength you receive by praying yes to God in private. When you feel weak, the quiet consistency of going to God will anchor you. Don't seek affirmation or sympathy from others; seek the quiet strength of your Father.

You cannot force your adult child to choose God. You cannot control their actions. But you can control the consistency of your witness. By refusing to compromise your values, you are offering the most powerful testimony you have left: that the faith you raised them with is real, firm, and worth more than anything on earth, including temporary peace. Hold the line, parent. The God of grace and truth is with you.

References

- John 1:14 (NASB)
- Ephesians 4:25 (NASB)
- Matthew 6:6 (NASB)

Historical and Anecdotal References:

Judas Maccabeus and the Hellenistic Compromise: The Maccabean Revolt and the refusal to compromise Jewish law under Greek pressure is a foundational example of religious integrity.

- o   *Reference: https://www.jewishvirtuallibrary.org/judas-maccabeus*

Charles Spurgeon Quote: "If there be but one point of the compass wrong..." The quote emphasizes the necessity of holding fast to pure doctrine.

- o   *Reference: https://www.spurgeon.org/resource-library/quotations/*

Reflection

Take a few minutes to reflect and meditate on what you just read. Write down your thoughts and take time to pray and praise God.

Day 5

Life Goes On

Life Goes On: Faith in the Now

When a major heartache hits—especially the pain of a broken relationship with an adult child—it feels like the world should just stop spinning. You wake up each and every day, and the grief is still there, heavy and real. It's natural to feel stuck, to want to put your life on hold until the situation is fixed, or to feel guilty about finding joy when your child is suffering or away.

But the truth is, life does go on. The sun comes up, your job still demands your attention, your spouse still needs your presence, and your other family and friends still need your love.

It can be a powerful act of faith to refuse to let grief paralyze you. Continuing to live your life fully—working, connecting with friends, serving others—is not a sign that you don't care about your child; it is a sign that you trust God with their future and with your present. It's about recognizing that God's plan for your sanctification (your growth in holiness) is happening right now, regardless of your child's choices.

The Danger of the Pause Button

When we put life on pause, we risk falling into the trap of making our child's situation the center of our universe, instead of God. This can lead to what we call "functional idolatry"—we start worshiping the idea of their return or the hope of a perfect family again, rather than worshiping the living God.

When your life is stuck, two things happen:

You Stop Growing: Your spiritual life stalls because you are so focused on a future outcome that you miss what God is doing in you today.

You Isolate: You pull away from the very people (spouse, friends, church community) who are meant to be your sources of strength and joy.

The Bible gives us a simple, and powerful command for how to live in the present. The Apostle Peter wrote to Christians who were facing severe trials, including scattering and persecution. He told them to look forward to the future, but to live faithfully in the present:

"Therefore, prepare your minds for action, keep sober in spirit, fix your hope completely on the grace to be brought to you at the revelation of Jesus Christ" (1 Peter 1:13, NASB).

Notice the action words: "prepare your minds for action." This isn't a call to sit and mourn indefinitely; it's a command to be spiritually and mentally ready for service. It means waking up and saying, "My child's path is in God's hands, and my life today is dedicated to His purpose."

Continuing to live, work, and love fully is an act of courageous obedience to God's ongoing call on your life.

Refocusing Your Race

When you are grieving, it often feels wrong to experience joy or success. You might cancel dinner plans, turn down volunteer opportunities, or even struggle to focus at work because the sorrow is so distracting. But these activities — work, family time, and friendship — are the tracks where God wants you to run your race.

1. The Necessity of Meaningful Work

Work, whether inside or outside the home, is one of the primary ways God gives us purpose and perspective. When you focus on a task, you are reminded that your worth isn't tied to your parenting results; it's tied to being a faithful steward of the gifts God has given you.

The wise King Solomon wrote: "Whatever your hand finds to do, verily, do it with all your might; for there is no activity or planning or knowledge or wisdom in Sheol where you are going" (Ecclesiastes 9:10, NASB).

This means that while you are here, alive and able, you must give your energy and focus to the tasks before you. Being faithful in your job, your volunteer role, or your daily duties and chores is a sacred act of service. It reminds you that your life has meaning beyond your single greatest heartache.

2. Guarding the Family You Still Have

When one relationship is broken, it can be tempting to neglect the other relationships, especially your spouse. Spouses often drift apart during periods of prolonged grief because they handle the pain differently, or because the absent child becomes the only topic of conversation.

It is absolutely crucial to turn toward your spouse, your other children, and your extended family during these difficult times.

Your spouse and family are a profound source of God's grace and stability.

The love and laughter you share with them is a gift from God that you are commanded to enjoy. "Behold, children are a gift of the Lord, the fruit of the womb is a reward" (Psalm 127:3, NASB). This verse is a reminder to cherish the family you have right now.

Make time for date nights, focus on the needs of your other children, and share moments of simple joy. This is not betrayal; it is stewardship of the blessings God has left in your care.

3. Re-engaging with Friends and Community

Isolation is the enemy of hope. When we isolate, our grief grows louder, and the lies of the enemy sound more convincing. Friends and your church community are the body of Christ designed to carry you through this trial.

The renowned humanitarian and Nobel Prize winner Albert Schweitzer once stated, "The purpose of human life is to serve, and to show compassion and the will to help others."

Your continued engagement with life, friends, and community allows you to receive help and, perhaps more importantly, to give help. When you shift your focus outward and serve someone else, your own burdens momentarily feel lighter.

Go have coffee with a friend, volunteer at your church, or simply sit in the pew next to other believers. Your community reminds you that you are part of a larger story than your current family crisis.

One of the things that we have done is focusing our time on serving on short term missions trips. This allows us to train and prepare to serve others (many times in third world or developing countries). It take the focus off of us and puts the focus on others.

Trusting God in the Unseen Future

Continuing to live means choosing trust over anxiety. You are choosing to believe that God's power and love for your child are active, even though you cannot see the results.

The Apostle Paul gives us a beautiful reminder that our current troubles are temporary compared to the glory that is coming: "For I consider that the sufferings of this present time are not worthy to be compared with the glory that is to be revealed to us" (Romans 8:18, NASB).

Your suffering today is real, but it is not the final word. The ability to embrace life, work, and community in the midst of this grief is a powerful testament to your trust in that future glory.

It is the quiet declaration that your heavenly Father is good, sovereign, and will never abandon your child or you.

Don't let your heartache steal your present. Live fully, love deeply, and trust completely.

References

- 1 Peter 1:13 (NASB)
- Ecclesiastes 9:10 (NASB)
- Psalm 127:3 (NASB)
- Romans 8:18 (NASB)

Historical and Anecdotal References:

Albert Schweitzer Quote: "The purpose of human life is to serve..." This quote reflects his lifelong commitment to service in Africa.

- *Reference: https://www.schweitzerfellowship.org/aboutus/albert-schweitzer*

Reflection

Take a few minutes to reflect and meditate on what you just read. Write down your thoughts and take time to pray and praise God.

_____
_____
_____
_____
_____
_____
_____
_____
_____
_____
_____
_____
_____
_____
_____

Day 6

Be at Peace

Be at Peace: Anchoring Your Soul in the Storm

When you are carrying the pain of a wayward adult child, you know that peace often feels like the most impossible thing to find. The daily worry, the sleepless nights, the sharp pangs of grief—they can all add up to a restless spirit. It's like living on a ship that is constantly being tossed by huge waves.

We often think that peace is the absence of trouble. We imagine that once our child is home, safe, and back in the faith, then we will finally feel peaceful.

But the peace God offers is different. It's not something you find when the storm is over; it's the anchor that holds your ship steady in the middle of the storm.

Jesus didn't promise us a life without trouble. Instead, He promised us this: "These things I have spoken to you, so that in Me you may have peace. In the world you have tribulation, but take courage; I have overcome the world" (John 16:33, NASB).

Jesus tells us two things here: You will have trouble (tribulation), but you can have peace. That peace is found only in Him. This chapter is about setting aside the chaotic noise of the world and the worry in your mind, and actively using the spiritual tools God gave us to experience His deep, steady peace right now.

The Four Pillars of Peace

Finding inner peace isn't just wishing for it; it's a deliberate spiritual practice. It requires engaging four key disciplines that work together to anchor your heart and mind to God.

1. The Anchor of Prayer: Handing Over the Battle

When you are deeply worried about your child, prayer often turns into frantic begging or demanding a specific outcome. But to find peace, prayer needs to become a surrender. It is the act of handing over the one thing you desperately want to control — your child's situation — to the only One who actually can control it.

The Apostle Paul gave us the direct formula for replacing anxiety with divine peace: "Do not be anxious about anything, but in everything by prayer and pleading with thanksgiving let your requests be made known to God. And the peace of God, which surpasses all comprehension, will guard your hearts and minds in Christ Jesus" (Philippians 4:6-7, NASB).

Notice the chain reaction:

You Stop Anxiety. You make a conscious decision to pause the worry.

You Start Thanksgiving. Even in the pain, you thank God for who He is — His goodness, His sovereignty, His love for your child. This is key!

The Result is Peace. The peace of God, which is so huge you can't even fully understand it, steps in and stands guard over your heart and mind.

This peace isn't logical from the worlds perspective!

It doesn't make sense that you could be peaceful while dealing with such grief. But that's why it's called the peace that "surpasses all comprehension" — it's supernatural, and it's only available when you trust God enough to genuinely surrender your worry in prayer.

2. The Comfort of Fellowship: Sharing the Burden

When you are hurting, the enemy loves to whisper that you are alone, that no one understands, and that you should hide your pain. Isolation is a thief of peace.

Fellowship — being with other believers — is where God intended for your burden to be shared and lightened.

It is where you find people who will stand in the gap with you in prayer and remind you of God's truth. The Bible clearly tells us that we are meant to carry each other's burdens: "Bear one another's burdens, and thereby fulfill the law of Christ" (Galatians 6:2, NASB).

Finding peace requires the humility to be honest about your own struggle with trusted Christian friends or your small group. When you open up, you allow others to fulfill "the law of Christ" by stepping in and sharing the weight of your worry. When you share the burden, it is instantly lighter.

Don't be too proud to let someone else stand under the weight with you for a while.

Our Sunday School class has been such a blessing for us as we have walked this path. They love us unconditionally and without any judgment. They laugh when we laugh and they cry when we cry. It's an amazing community of believers.

3. **The Clarity of Biblical Study: Realigning Your Mind**

Anxiety is often fueled by thinking about "what-ifs." To replace that chaos with peace, you must fill your mind with God's unchanging "what-is." The "what-is" is the truth found only in the Bible.

Biblical study is the act of intentionally recalibrating your mind to God's perspective, especially when your emotions are running wild.

When you are worried about your child's security, you read verses about God's protection. When you doubt His love, you read about the Cross. This constant infusion of truth pushes out fear.

The Psalmist captured this perfectly, noting that God's Word is the source of inner stability: "Those who love Your law have great peace, and nothing causes them to stumble" (Psalm 119:165, NASB).

Peace is the result of aligning your thoughts with God's Word. When your child's life looks messy and hopeless, reading the Bible reminds you of God's history of restoration. It reminds you that God delights in using what looks broken and impossible to display His amazing power.

4. **The Release of Worship: Fixing Your Gaze**

Worship is perhaps the most powerful tool for finding immediate peace.

Worship is simply the act of giving God the value and praise He deserves, regardless of your current circumstances. When you sing, pray, or meditate on the greatness of God, you are essentially telling your anxiety: "You are not bigger than the God I serve."

Historically, people of great faith have always turned to worship in their deepest trials. Consider the hymn writer Fanny Crosby (1820–1915). She was blinded in infancy, yet she wrote thousands of hymns that are filled with confidence, joy, and peace in God. She didn't have an easy life, but she chose to focus on God's greatness, writing classic hymns like "Blessed Assurance."

In one of her famous writings, she said, "O what a happy soul I am, although I cannot see. I am resolved that in this world, contentment shall be my lot." Her peace was not based on her sight, but on her focus — on worshipping the unseen God.

When you worship, you shift your gaze from the huge, looming problem (your child's situation) to the huge, unchanging person (God). You are literally magnifying God, which makes your problem shrink in comparison.

The Legacy of Peace

Finding this peace is not just for your own comfort; it's also a powerful witness.

The famous Swiss psychiatrist and philosopher Carl Jung understood that inner conflict is damaging to the whole person. He noted, "Man cannot stand a meaningless life. When you find your peace in God, you declare that your life, even in this pain, is not meaningless."

The peace you demonstrate is the most compelling argument you can offer to your child and to the world that your faith is real.

When your child sees your love for them is unwavering, yet your inner stability is not dependent on their choices, they see the supernatural power of Christ at work.

You are not fighting for peace; you are receiving it as a gift from the Holy Spirit. "But the fruit of the Spirit is love, joy, peace, patience, kindness, goodness, faithfulness, gentleness, self-control; against such things there is no law" (Galatians 5:22–23, NASB).

Peace is a fruit that God grows in you as you lean on Him through prayer, fellowship, study, and worship. Commit to cultivating these four pillars every day.

Trust that the anchor holds, and be at peace.

References

- John 16:33 (NASB)
- Philippians 4:6–7 (NASB)
- Galatians 6:2 (NASB)
- Psalm 119:165 (NASB)
- Galatians 5:22–23 (NASB)

Historical and Anecdotal References:

Fanny Crosby: Her life story and quote emphasize finding contentment and peace despite blindness and hardship.

- *Reference: https://www.christianitytoday.com/history/people/musicians/fanny-crosby.html*

Carl Jung Quote: "Man cannot stand a meaningless life." The quote reflects his observations on the human need for purpose and inner order.

- *Reference: https://www.carl-jung.net/quotes.html*

Reflection

Take a few minutes to reflect and meditate on what you just read. Write down your thoughts and take time to pray and praise God.

Day 7

Take Every Thought Captive

Taking Every Thought Captive: The Battle for Your Mind

If you've been on this journey of loving a wayward adult child for any length of time, you know the war isn't just external; it's a war waged in your own head. It is a war that never seems to end.

You might be lying awake at 3 a.m. when your mind turns into a terrible movie projector, replaying all the mistakes you think you made as a parent. Or maybe a casual conversation triggers a wave of fear about your child's future, sending you into a spiral of "what-ifs."

The enemy knows that if he can control your thoughts, he can steal your peace, your joy, and eventually, your hope.

This is why the Apostle Paul gave us one of the most powerful and practical commands in the Bible: "We are taking every thought captive to the obedience of Christ" (2 Corinthians 10:5, NASB).

Notice Paul doesn't say, "Wait for the bad thoughts to go away." He says "taking every thought captive." This is an active, aggressive, military term. It means you must treat every negative, fearful, untrue, or condemning thought as an enemy combatant that you must arrest, disarm, and surrender to the authority of Christ.

This chapter is about learning to fight the battle for your mind so that you can dwell on God's faithfulness, not your own fear.

The Thought Factory

Our minds are like factories that never stop running. Every day, they produce thousands of thoughts—some helpful, some harmless, and many that are outright destructive. When you are under the stress of a child walking away, the factory tends to go into overdrive producing toxic thoughts:

Regret and Guilt: "It's my fault. If I had done X, this wouldn't have happened."

Fear and Catastrophe: "They will never come back. They will end up homeless or in jail."

Worry and Analysis: Endless mental replaying of conversations, searching for clues or ways to fix the situation.

These thoughts are the static we talked about in earlier chapters. They prevent you from hearing God and drain the strength you need to live a peaceful life. You cannot control what thoughts initially pop into your head, but you can control where those thoughts are allowed to dwell.

The Wisdom of a Disciplined Mind

Throughout history, wise leaders have recognized that the mind is the key to victory, peace, and leadership.

The ancient Roman Emperor Marcus Aurelius, a man who carried the heavy burden of ruling an empire, understood that inner discipline was everything. He wrote in his Meditations: "You have power over your mind—not outside events. Realize this, and you will find strength."

As Christians, we know this power comes not from our own willpower, but from the Holy Spirit. But Aurelius's point is still true: We have power over our minds. Our strength lies in choosing to discipline our thoughts and refuse to dwell on the "outside events" that we cannot control (like our child's decisions).

The Four-Step Capture Plan

Taking a thought captive is not a complicated process, but it requires consistency. Here is a practical, four-step plan to fight the battle in your mind.

1. Identify and Intercept

The moment a negative, fearful, or self-condemning thought enters your awareness, you must intercept it. Don't let it unpack its bags and move into your mind.

Example: The thought flashes, "I failed as a parent."

Action: Immediately stop and say aloud or in your heart, "Stop. This thought is not from God."

This is the "taking captive" part. You recognize the thought, identify it as a threat to your faith, and immediately halt its progress.

2. Challenge and Check the Source

Once you've intercepted the thought, you need to challenge its truthfulness and check it against the ultimate authority: the Bible.

Most toxic thoughts are not true, or they are only partially true, twisted with lies.

The Lie: "I failed as a parent." (A toxic, condemning thought.)

The Challenge: Did I do my best with the knowledge I had? Am I defined by my child's choices or by Christ's redemption?

The Truth Check: The Bible says, "There is now no condemnation for those who are in Christ Jesus" (Romans 8:1, NASB). Your worth is not based on your performance, but on Christ's finished work.

This second step disarms the thought. You replace the lie with God's unchanging truth.

3. **Replace with God's Focus**

You cannot simply empty your mind; you must refill it with something true and pure. The space where the fearful thought used to be needs to be immediately planted with a thought of God's faithfulness.

Paul tells us exactly what kind of thought should be allowed to dwell in our minds: "Finally, brothers and sisters, whatever is true, whatever is honorable, whatever is right, whatever is pure, whatever is lovely, whatever is of good repute, if there is any excellence and if anything worthy of praise, dwell on these things" (Philippians 4:8, NASB).

When the fearful thought about your child's future is arrested, you replace it by dwelling on God's goodness:

Replacement Thought: "It is true that my child is struggling, but God is faithful. It is honorable to trust Him. It is lovely that He loves my child more than I do."

Action: Re-direct your thoughts to focus on a memory of God's past faithfulness in your life, or recite a short Bible verse about His goodness.

4. **Put on the Helmet of Salvation**

This entire battle is a spiritual war, and we need spiritual armor.

Paul describes the importance of protecting your mind in Ephesians: "And take THE HELMET OF SALVATION, and the sword of the Spirit, which is the word of God" (Ephesians 6:17, NASB).

The Helmet of Salvation protects you from the attacks that try to shake your confidence in who you are in Christ. When the enemy whispers, "You are a failure," the Helmet reminds you, "I am saved, redeemed, and fully accepted by God." When he whispers, "Your situation is hopeless," the Helmet reminds you, "My hope is in Christ, who overcame the world."

The battle for your mind is a daily, sometimes hourly, commitment. But every time you successfully take a thought captive and replace it with God's truth, you gain strength, you gain peace, and you honor God by choosing to focus on His infinite power rather than your limited fears.

References

- 2 Corinthians 10:5 (NASB)
- Romans 8:1 (NASB)
- Philippians 4:8 (NASB)
- Ephesians 6:17 (NASB)

Historical and Anecdotal References:

Marcus Aurelius Quote: "You have power over your mind—not outside events. Realize this, and you will find strength," from Meditations, one of the most famous works of Stoic philosophy.

  o *Reference: https://classics.mit.edu/Antoninus/meditations.html*

Reflection

Take a few minutes to reflect and meditate on what you just read. Write down your thoughts and take time to pray and praise God.

_____
_____
_____
_____
_____
_____
_____
_____
_____
_____
_____
_____
_____
_____
_____

Day 8

Seek Wise Counsel

Seeking Wise Counsel: Finding Light in the Confusion

When you are deeply worried about your adult child, your mind can feel like a tangled mess of fear, guilt, and exhaustion.

In those moments, it's almost impossible to see the road ahead clearly.

Every decision—when to talk, when to send a text, when to draw a boundary—feels weighted and huge.

It is during these seasons of intense stress and confusion that we are most in danger of making decisions based on raw emotion instead of biblical wisdom. This is why we need to intentionally step outside of our own heads and seek the perspective of wise, godly counsel.

Seeking counsel is not a sign that your faith is weak; it is a sign that your humility is strong. It means you trust God enough to believe that He often speaks His wisdom to you through other people.

The Danger of Going It Alone

When a child walks away, many parents feel intense shame and isolation. The natural tendency is to pull back, tell no one, and try to manage the crisis in secret.

This is spiritually dangerous.

When you try to walk this path alone, you are relying solely on your own limited strength and perspective.

The Bible warns against this isolation. The book of Proverbs, which is full of practical wisdom, highlights the power of shared counsel: "Without consultation, plans go awry, but with many counselors they succeed" (Proverbs 15:22, NASB).

When you are in deep pain, your own "plans" (like how to talk to your child, or how to handle a crisis) are likely to "go awry" because they are being fueled by these intense feelings.

Getting "many counselors" means you invite trusted, grounded people into your situation so they can help you see the blind spots you are missing. A blind spot by definition is something you cannot see!

This counsel isn't just about getting advice; it's about getting accountability and gaining perspective.

Discerning True Wisdom

Beware!! Not all counsel is helpful.

When you are hurting, you might accidentally seek out people who will simply sympathize with you, or who will agree with whatever angry or anxious feelings you have. Sympathy is nice, but it's not the same as wise counsel.

True wise counsel must meet three crucial criteria:

1. It Must Be Rooted in Scripture

The most important source of wisdom is always God's Word.

Any person who claims to be giving you Christian counsel, but whose advice contradicts the Bible, should not be trusted.

For instance, if they advise you to compromise your faith to keep your child happy, they are giving you human comfort, not godly wisdom.

The counsel you seek must honor God first, even if it feels difficult for you and your child. Scripture says that God's law brings understanding, even to the simple: "The testimony of the Lord is sure, making wise the simple"

(Psalm 19:7, NASB). The person you seek advice from should use the Bible to bring clarity to your simple, overwhelmed mind.

I know if our case, when we were dealing with some issues with one of our prodigal children, we sought out "wise counsel". We had some friends who pointed us in the direction of "experts" and other parents who had similar experiences to ours but were supposedly much more grounded "wise".

The "so called experts" told us that we should just basically accept the situation, that it was not going to change and we needed to adapt and better understand our child.

These "experienced parents" had basically given up and given in and completed accommodated their child and accepted the choices they were making so they could have peace and harmony and a relationship with their child.

We could not accept either of the choices because it would have caused us to compromise our faith and values. Do we want and desire peace and tranquility – yes of course! But not at this cost!

Be very careful whose advice you take, whether live or served up to you on the internet.

2. It Must Come from Proven Character

Look for counselors who have successfully navigated major life storms while remaining faithful to God.

Don't just look for successful people; look for enduring people. Their advice is seasoned by their own history of trusting God when it was hard.

As the great abolitionist and statesman Abraham Lincoln often relied on his cabinet and trusted advisors during the Civil War, he understood that the weight of a crisis requires sharing the load with individuals of established integrity and proven judgment. He was known to seek out perspectives that challenged his own, knowing that truth often emerges from thoughtful disagreement.

Look for people who:

- ✓ Have long-lasting marriages and stable family lives (if applicable).
- ✓ Demonstrate patience and peace in their own personal struggles.
- ✓ Are quick to listen and slow to speak (James 1:19).

3. It Must Be Consistent and Confirmed

If you seek counsel from three different, godly people, and they all offer the same basic direction, then that is a pretty good and strong indicator that you are getting sound advice. If you get wildly different advice from everyone, you need to slow down and pray more before moving forward.

Also, be sure your spouse is your primary counselor and co-laborer during this journey.

Finally, you must be united with your spouse in what you share with others and what decisions you make regarding your child. If you are married, seeking counsel outside of your spouse is dangerous; you must be a team in this challenge.

Where to Find Wise Counsel
Where do you actually go to get this kind of help? You should look for several different types of resources to provide you with a well-rounded perspective.

1. Trusted Church Leaders (Pastors/Elders)

Your spiritual leaders have often seen similar situations and have training in providing biblical guidance. They can offer a high-level, theological perspective on your child's spiritual battle and help you frame your pain within God's overall plan.

2. Qualified Christian Counselors

Sometimes, the pain and trauma are too deep for a simple conversation. A licensed Christian counselor or therapist can help you untangle the psychological knots of guilt, regret, and anxiety. They are trained to help you process your grief and establish necessary emotional boundaries, helping you implement the peace that we discussed in the last chapter. They often provide a neutral, safe space free from judgment.

3. Experienced Friends/Mentors

Look for an older couple or a mentor in your church who has successfully navigated the challenges of raising adult children, especially those who have faced difficulties.

They can offer an anecdotal, real-life perspective.

They can tell you what worked, what didn't, and, most importantly, they can offer enduring hope: "We got through this, and you can too." The will also pray with you and pray for you through the trials and tribulations.

The purpose of seeking counsel is not to shift the burden of decision-making, but to clarify your own heart and mind so that you can make the decision with courage and confidence.

When you move forward with the confirmed wisdom of Godly counsel, you can rest knowing you did not move alone. You stood with God, and with the body of Christ.

References

- Proverbs 15:22 (NASB)
- Psalm 19:7 (NASB)
- Galatians 6:2 (NASB)
- James 1:19 (Implied in the description of character)

Historical and Anecdotal References:

Abraham Lincoln and the Civil War Cabinet: Lincoln's reliance on his "team of rivals" and trusted advisors is a historical example of seeking wide counsel during a crisis.

- *Reference: https://www.archives.gov/publications/prologue/2005/winter/lincoln-cabinet.html*

Reflection

Take a few minutes to reflect and meditate on what you just read. Write down your thoughts and take time to pray and praise God.

Day 9

Beware of Bitterness and Envy

Guarding Your Heart: Trading Bitterness for Blessing

When your heart is hurting over your adult child, it's natural to start looking around at other families.

You see the Facebook photos of your friend's child graduating with honors, getting a great job, or getting married in a beautiful ceremony, and a tight, ugly knot forms in your stomach.

You see another family that seems perfectly happy and spiritually successful, and you think, "Why them? Why not us?"

This is the sneaky, destructive path of bitterness and envy.

Bitterness is anger that has settled down and made a home in your heart. Envy is the deep, unhappy longing for someone else's good fortune, which then leads to resenting them for having it.

It is that bitterness is like taking poison, but expecting the other person to die!

These emotions are toxic. They don't hurt the people you envy; they only poison your own soul and block the flow of God's peace.

This chapter is about learning to recognize the roots of these feelings and actively trading them for the assurance of God's personal goodness to you.

The Root of Bitterness

Bitterness often grows from feeling cheated by God.

We feel that we played by the rules—we raised our children in the church, taught them the Bible, and tried our best—and yet we didn't get the "reward" of a successful, faithful family. When we see others who seem to have that reward easily, our heart asks, "Why did God choose to bless them and not me?"

This is a dangerous place to be because it attacks the very core of God's character: His goodness.

The book of Hebrews gives us a strong warning about the danger of letting this root take hold: "See to it that no one comes short of the grace of God; that no root of bitterness springing up causes trouble, and by it many be defiled" (Hebrews 12:15, NASB).

The Bible calls bitterness a "root." A root is hidden deep underground, but its effect—the visible, poisonous plant—causes trouble and defiles the whole area. If you let bitterness stay, it will contaminate your marriage, your relationships with your other children, your church life, and your relationship with God.

The only way to pull out this root is to replace the lie—God is unfair—with the truth—God is faithful.

The Foolishness of Comparison

Envy is born from the foolish habit of comparing your life's internal struggles to someone else's external presentation. We compare our backstage chaos to someone else's front-row seats.

The truth is, you don't know the full story of the family you are envying.

Their "successful" child might be facing deep, hidden struggles, or that perfect-looking couple might be dealing with a crisis you know nothing about.

The Bible warns us against this kind of measurement: "For we are not bold to classify or compare ourselves with some of those who commend themselves; but when they measure themselves by themselves and compare themselves with themselves, they are without understanding" (2 Corinthians 10:12, NASB).

Paul says this kind of comparison is "without understanding." It is a misunderstanding of how God works. Your worth, your success, and your blessings are not measured against the person next to you; they are measured only by the grace and calling of God for your life.

The Lesson from the Laborers

Jesus told a parable that speaks directly to envy: the Parable of the Laborers (Matthew 20:1-16). In the story, a landowner hires workers at different times of the day. But when it's time to pay them, he gives the same pay—a denarius—to everyone, including those who only worked for an hour.

The workers who worked all day were instantly envious of those who worked less: "When they received it, they grumbled at the landowner, saying, 'These last men have worked only one hour, and you have made them equal to us who have borne the burden of the day and the scorching heat'" (Matthew 20:11-12, NASB).

The landowner responds with a direct, challenging question: "'Is it not lawful for me to do what I wish with what is my own? Or is your eye envious because I am generous?'" (Matthew 20:15, NASB).

This is a powerful lesson: God is the generous Owner.

He chooses how to bless, when to bless, and who to bless. When we are envious, we are essentially grumbling at God's right to be generous to someone else.

Our eyes are "envious" because we think God's generosity should have a ceiling based on our perceived effort.

Trading Bitterness for Blessing

The only way to eliminate bitterness and envy is through gratitude and contentment. You must actively choose to focus on the blessings God has given you that are not tied to your child's choices.

1. **Actively Practice Gratitude**

Gratitude is the spiritual disinfectant for bitterness.

When you feel that knot of envy, immediately stop and intentionally list three things God has done for you today or in the past year. This isn't about ignoring your pain, but about recognizing that your life is still overwhelmingly full of God's grace.

The Apostle Paul commands us to pray with thanksgiving, which is the direct antidote to worry and bitterness: "in everything by prayer and pleading with thanksgiving let your requests be made known to God" (Philippians 4:6, NASB).

2. **Recognize Your Unique Calling**

Your story is unique.

Your struggles are unique.

And the way God is using you to demonstrate faithfulness in the midst of pain is unique and powerful. Your calling is not to have the perfect family, but to trust and glorify God in your reality.

The great Christian philosopher and theologian Saint Augustine understood that peace is found when our desires align with God's reality. He famously prayed, "You have made us for yourself, O Lord, and our hearts are restless until they find their rest in you."

When you envy another family's peace, you miss the rest that God has for your heart.

Your rest is found not in changing your external circumstances, but in surrendering your internal resentment and resting in God's plan for your family, imperfect as it currently is.

3. Pray for the Person You Envy

This is the hardest, but most effective step. When you feel envy toward another parent's situation, immediately turn that feeling into a prayer of blessing for them.

Action: "Lord, I confess I feel jealous of their peace. Please bless that family. Thank You for the good things You are doing in their lives. And Lord, I ask that You show me the good things You are doing in mine."

This breaks the power of the enemy.

It replaces your toxic focus with God's command to love and bless others. By choosing to bless, you tear down the wall of bitterness in your heart and open yourself up to receive the specific, personal blessings God has reserved just for you.

References

- Hebrews 12:15 (NASB)
- 2 Corinthians 10:12 (NASB)
- Matthew 20:11-12 (NASB)
- Matthew 20:15 (NASB)
- Philippians 4:6 (NASB)

Historical and Anecdotal References:

Saint Augustine Quote: "You have made us for yourself, O Lord..." from his Confessions.

- *Reference: https://www.ccel.org/ccel/augustine/confessions.iv.html*

Paul Beersdorf

Reflection

Take a few minutes to reflect and meditate on what you just read. Write down your thoughts and take time to pray and praise God.

Paul Beersdorf

Day 10

Fellowship

Stay Connected: The Power of Community in Crisis

When you are walking through the deep, ongoing pain of a wayward adult child, one of the first things you might feel tempted to do is disappear.

You might skip church because you don't want to smile and pretend everything is fine. You might avoid your small group because you can't face the questions or the thought of hearing someone else's good news. You think, "I just need to deal with this alone."

But isolation is exactly what the enemy wants. When you separate yourself from the community of believers, you cut yourself off from the very lifelines God designed to keep you afloat during a storm.

This chapter is a reminder that maintaining fellowship and worship with other Christians isn't just a good idea—it is a spiritual necessity for survival and healing.

The Danger of Isolation

Think of a burning coal.

If it stays in the fire with other coals, it burns bright and hot. But if you pull that one coal away from the pile, it quickly loses its heat and turns cold and gray.

Your faith is the same way. When you pull away from Christian fellowship, your spiritual passion and energy quickly fade.

The Bible is crystal clear about the importance of staying connected. The writer of Hebrews gives us a direct command about protecting our community, especially when life is difficult:

"And let us consider how to stimulate one another to love and good deeds, not forsaking our own assembling together, as is the habit of some, but encouraging one another; and all the more as you see the day drawing near" (Hebrews 10:24-25, NASB).

Notice two key phrases:

"Not forsaking our own assembling together." The church isn't just a place to go; it's a place where you are spiritually protected and energized. Skipping out isn't just missing a service; it's refusing the encouragement God has prepared for you.

"Encouraging one another." You are called to be both a giver and a receiver of encouragement. When you show up, you are blessed by others, and you bless others just by being a faithful example of endurance.

Staying connected helps you realize that your suffering is not unique, and that you are surrounded by people who will pray for you without judgment.

Fellowship: Shared Strength for Shared Burdens

Fellowship is more than just polite conversation after the service. It's the deep, honest sharing of life's struggles. It is where we put into practice the "one anothers" of the Bible — we instruct one another, pray for one another, and most importantly, bear one another's burdens.

The Apostle Paul wrote: "Bear one another's burdens, and thereby fulfill the law of Christ" (Galatians 6:2, NASB).

When you are grieving, your burden feels too heavy to carry alone.

Finding a trusted friend or a small group where you can truly be honest is like offloading a huge weight onto a team of people. It doesn't mean your problem goes away, but the weight no longer crushes you.

Wise Counsel and Accountability:

As we discussed in the last chapter, wise counsel is found in fellowship. Your church community provides the accountability you need to stop falling into the traps of bitterness, envy, and isolation.

When a trusted friend asks you how you are really doing, it forces you to capture those toxic thoughts before they take root.

Worship: Shifting the Focus

Worship is the powerful discipline of deliberately turning your focus away from the chaos of your circumstances and toward the constancy of God's character.

When your heart is breaking, the act of singing hymns, listening to teaching, or sharing communion is not about feeling happy; it is an act of spiritual defiance.

Worship declares: "Even though my life is in ruins, my God is still on the throne."

When you engage in corporate (group) worship, your faith is strengthened by the faith of those around you.

When your own voice might feel weak or your feelings numb, standing next to others who are singing truths about God's faithfulness acts as a spiritual transfusion. Their belief helps to reinforce your own when your tank is empty.

A powerful example of this focus comes from the history of music. The great composer Johann Sebastian Bach (1685–1750), a deeply religious man who faced tremendous personal hardship, including the early deaths of several of his children, viewed all his musical work as worship. He often signed his compositions "Soli Deo Gloria" — "Glory to God Alone."

Bach didn't let his personal sorrow stop him from creating and offering his life's work as praise. He understood that regardless of his feelings or circumstances, God's worth was unchanging.

When we worship, we are echoing Bach's declaration: We give glory to God alone, putting aside the pain of our parenting struggles, even if just for an hour.

Fellowship as a Mark of Endurance

For Christian parents in your situation, your consistent presence in fellowship and worship, even while grieving, is a profound statement. It is a powerful example of endurance to your other family members, your church, and even to your own heart.

The Apostle Paul encourages the believers in Rome with this call to steady hope and community involvement: "Rejoice in hope, be patient in tribulation, be constant in prayer, contributing to the needs of the saints, practicing hospitality" (Romans 12:12-13, NASB).

Notice how prayer (personal), tribulation (painful waiting), and contributing/hospitality (fellowship) are all listed together. You cannot do one without the others. Being patient in tribulation requires the constant refueling that comes from participating in the life of the church and serving others.

When you refuse to isolate, you are effectively telling your pain that it will not win. You are declaring that your identity is tied not to the outcome of your child's journey, but to the indestructible Body of Christ. You belong. You are loved. You are supported.

Choose today to stay connected.

Choose the warm, sometimes messy, light of the fellowship over the cold, deceiving darkness of isolation. Your strength for the marathon ahead depends on it.

References

- Hebrews 10:24-25 (NASB)
- Galatians 6:2 (NASB)
- Romans 12:12-13 (NASB)

Historical and Anecdotal References:

Johann Sebastian Bach (Soli Deo Gloria): His practice of dedicating his music to God alone, despite personal tragedy, is a classical example of worshipful focus during hardship.

- *Reference: https://www.bachvereniging.nl/en/all-of-bach/soli-deo-gloria*

Reflection

Take a few minutes to reflect and meditate on what you just read. Write down your thoughts and take time to pray and praise God.

Day 11

Friends

Friends Are the Family You Choose: The Power of Peer Support

In the difficult, ongoing journey of loving a wayward adult child, you need more than just family; you need friends.

Friends offer a unique kind of support. They are the people who know your history, who love you for who you are, and who often don't have the same emotional baggage or intense investment in your child's outcome that your immediate family does.

They can give you a vital sense of normalcy and perspective.

However, when grief hits, it's easy to pull away from friends.

You might feel too tired to socialize, or too embarrassed to share your pain, or too afraid of hearing their parenting successes compared to your struggles. But maintaining these friendships isn't a luxury; it's a necessity for your spiritual and emotional health.

This chapter is about understanding the different roles Christian friends play in carrying your burden and intentionally prioritizing that fellowship to keep your soul steady.

The Gift of the Outer Circle

Think of your life raft. Your spouse is the floor, and your other children are the walls—they hold the structure together. Your friends are the life preservers floating right alongside you, keeping you from sinking entirely.

The Bible emphasizes the tremendous value of true friendship, especially in times of distress. A proverb often attributed to King Solomon speaks beautifully to the enduring strength of a loyal friend: "A friend loves at all times, and a brother is born for adversity" (Proverbs 17:17, NASB).

A friend loves you "at all times," not just when things are going well. And sometimes, the friends you choose become the **"brother...born for adversity"—**the steady, loyal companion God provides specifically for the hard seasons of life.

When you allow friends into your pain, they do two things for you:

They provide perspective. They can gently remind you that your entire identity is not defined by this one crisis.

They provide distraction. They can give you moments of genuine, guilt-free joy that allow your brain and heart to rest from the cycle of worry.

Discerning Different Kinds of Friends

Not every friend can carry this specific burden, and that's okay. You need to discern which friends fill which roles in your life, seeking different types of support from different people.

1. The Confidante (The Burden Bearer)

This is the friend (or friends) with whom you can be completely honest about your child, your doubts, and your fears.

They are trustworthy, they are grounded in Christ, and they are committed to prayer. This is the friend who helps you "bear one another's burdens" (Galatians 6:2, NASB).

When seeking out a Confidante, look for someone who:

Listens More Than They Talk: They don't try to fix it; they simply sit in the pain with you.

Speaks Truth, Not Just Sympathy: They will remind you of God's faithfulness, even if it's hard to hear.

2. The Encourager (The Joy Giver)

This is the friend who helps you live the "life goes on" chapter.

They are your movie buddy, your workout partner, or your coffee date. They are the person who forces you to smile, laugh, and engage with the world outside your grief.

These friends help you fulfill the command to practice gratitude even amid tribulation: "Rejoice always; pray without ceasing; in everything give thanks; for this is God's will for you in Christ Jesus" (1 Thessalonians 5:16–18, NASB).

This friend reminds you that joy is not betrayal; it is a weapon against despair. It is a necessary act of spiritual self-care to allow yourself to experience lightness and laughter.

3. The Accountability Partner (The Truth Keeper)

This friend helps you take every thought captive.

They are the person you can ask, "Am I becoming bitter? Am I isolating myself too much? Am I being judgmental?" They hold you accountable to the commitments you made in earlier chapters—to stay peaceful and to keep showing up.

The Bible praises this kind of honest, challenging friendship: "Iron sharpens iron, so one person sharpens another" (Proverbs 27:17, NASB). This friend isn't just nice; they are sharpening you, helping you maintain the edge of your faith through honest feedback.

Simple Steps to Stay Connected

You don't need elaborate plans to maintain these connections. When you are exhausted, simple acts of reaching out are enough.

1. Be Honest about Your Capacity

When a friend invites you out, don't just say "no." Be honest about your energy level. You can say, "I'm not up for a dinner party, but could you come over for fifteen minutes of tea? I just need to see a friendly face." This manages their expectations while still allowing you to receive support.

2. Practice Reciprocity

Remember that friendship is a two-way street.

Your friends have struggles, too. Even in your pain, ask a friend how they are doing and genuinely listen.

When you shift your focus outward and pray for your friends' needs, you take the focus off your own problem and fulfill the command to "look out not only for his own interests, but also for the interests of others" (Philippians 2:4, NASB).

3. Schedule the Connection

When life is chaotic, connection must be scheduled.

Commit to one weekly touch point—a phone call, a standing coffee date, or a video chat. If you wait until you feel like reaching out, you may never do it.

The great humanitarian and Nobel Peace Prize winner Mother Teresa understood that true service and love require persistence and focus, which often come through strong community. She said, "Loneliness and the feeling of being unwanted is the most terrible poverty."

Do not let the loneliness of this trial become your poverty. Reach out to your friends. Allow their love, laughter, and wisdom to lift you up. By prioritizing your friends, you are accepting the strength God wants to give you through the people He put in your life.

References

- Proverbs 17:17 (NASB)
- Galatians 6:2 (NASB)
- 1 Thessalonians 5:16–18 (NASB)
- Proverbs 27:17 (NASB)
- Philippians 2:4 (NASB)

Historical and Anecdotal References:

Mother Teresa Quote: "Loneliness and the feeling of being unwanted is the most terrible poverty." This quote reflects her deep understanding of human need and connection.

- *Reference: https://www.motherteresa.org/*

Reflection

Take a few minutes to reflect and meditate on what you just read. Write down your thoughts and take time to pray and praise God.

_____
_____
_____
_____
_____
_____
_____
_____
_____
_____
_____
_____
_____
_____
_____
_____
_____
_____
_____

Day 12

Family

The Inner Circle: Cultivating Your Family Lifeline

When a deep crisis hits your family, like a child walking away, it creates a powerful emotional vacuum.

The worry is so intense that it can suck all the energy and focus away from your other, vital relationships—especially your spouse, your remaining children, and your extended family.

It's natural to let the missing piece of the family puzzle become your entire focus. However, if you let the crisis with your wayward child drain the life out of your marriage and your relationships with your other children, you risk turning one broken relationship into a chain reaction of breaks.

This chapter is about protecting and prioritizing your Inner Circle—the family unit God has blessed you with today.

Loving your missing child doesn't mean neglecting the ones who are still standing right beside you. Your enduring love and commitment to your Inner Circle are acts of faith, proving that the foundation of your home remains secure in Christ.

Protecting the Primary Vow: Your Spouse

For married parents, your marriage is the absolute most important human relationship in your life.

It is the primary place where you find refuge and shared strength. But grief and worry are incredibly tough on a marriage. Spouses often handle the pain of a wayward child differently—one might want to talk constantly, while the other retreats into silence. This difference can quickly lead to painful isolation.

The Bible makes it clear that your spouse is your life partner in faith, not just your parenting partner: "Two are better than one because they have a good return for their labor. For if either of them falls, the one will lift up his companion. But woe to the one who falls when there is not another to lift him up" (Ecclesiastes 4:9–10, NASB).

You and your spouse are a team lifting each other up. To protect your marriage, you must:

Communicate, Don't Criticize:

Share your feelings and fears about your child, but never criticize how your spouse is coping or handling the situation. You are on the same team, even if you are processing the pain differently.

Prioritize Time Together:

Make time for date nights, quiet evenings, or just an hour where you intentionally talk about things other than your wayward child. You need reminders of why you fell in love and how strong your foundation is.

Pray Together:

This is the most unifying act you can perform. Praying together for your child and for each other ensures that you are both relying on the same source of strength.

Cherishing the Present: Your Other Children

It can be tragically easy to let the missing child cast a shadow over the children who are still present in your home and life.

Your other sons and daughters need to know two things clearly:

1. They are loved unconditionally. They should never feel that the emotional crisis surrounding their sibling somehow diminishes their own worth or their parents' focus on them.

2. They are not replacements. They must not feel pressured to be "extra good" or overly spiritual to make up for their sibling's choices.

Your other children are looking to you to see how a mature Christian handles profound pain.

Your ability to find joy, maintain healthy routines, and celebrate their successes, even while grieving the absent one, is a powerful lesson in faithfulness and endurance.

The Psalmist reminds us to cherish the blessing of family: "Behold, children are a gift of the Lord, the fruit of the womb is a reward" (Psalm 127:3, NASB). This verse is a call to actively cherish the reward you have today.

Set aside specific, technology-free time with your other children.

Go to their events, ask about their lives, and allow yourself to laugh and experience simple joy with them. Doing so honors the gift of family that God has preserved for you.

Drawing Strength from the Extended Family Tree

Your siblings, aunts, uncles, and in-laws form a crucial extended support system. They are the people who share your history and understand your family's heart without needing a long explanation.

When seeking support from your extended family, it's important to set healthy expectations:

Be Specific: Don't just suffer silently. Ask for what you need: "Would you pray for my marriage this week?" or "Can you call me on Thursday? I just need to laugh."

Protect Confidentiality: Be mindful of what you share and who you share it with, especially information about your wayward child. Extended family support should be about supporting you, not gossiping about your child.

Be Open to Reciprocity: Your job in fellowship is not just to receive; it is to give. When you allow yourself to be a resource of support and love to them — listening to their troubles or helping them with a need — you refocus your energy outward, which is incredibly healing.

The American author and activist Helen Keller, who faced tremendous physical isolation due to blindness and deafness, spoke profoundly about the power of connection: "Alone we can do so little; together we can do so much."

This is the principle of the Christian family: You cannot carry this burden alone.

By intentionally drawing near to your spouse, your children, and your supportive relatives, you create a powerful, multi-layered defense against isolation and despair. You are not just surviving; you are strengthening the foundation of your faith and your home for the future.

References

- Ecclesiastes 4:9–10 (NASB)
- Psalm 127:3 (NASB)

Historical and Anecdotal References:

Helen Keller Quote: "Alone we can do so little; together we can do so much." This quote reflects her reliance on her intimate support system (like her teacher, Annie Sullivan) to achieve her life's work.

- o   *Reference: https://www.afb.org/about-us/helen-keller*

Reflection

Take a few minutes to reflect and meditate on what you just read. Write down your thoughts and take time to pray and praise God.

Day 13
Self-Control

Self-Control: Finding Calm in the Chaos

If you are a parent of a wayward adult child, the most frequent feeling you probably experience is powerlessness. You feel like everything is spinning out of your control: your child's life, the family dynamic, and your own emotional state.

When you feel powerless, your natural human reaction is to lash out or try to over-control the few things you can touch — which often leads to emotional outbursts, giving in to destructive habits (like overeating or excessive worry), or pushing too hard on your child and creating more distance.

The good news is that God has equipped you with a powerful tool to handle this chaos: self-control.

This isn't just about willpower; it is a supernatural fruit of the Holy Spirit. Exercising self-control is your way of declaring, "My internal life is governed by God, not by my external circumstances."

This chapter will focus on how to activate this spiritual muscle to bring calm and stability back into your life, even when everything else feels out of control.

The Source of Inner Discipline

It's tempting to think that strong self-control belongs only to super-disciplined people, but for the Christian, it is a guaranteed gift from God. The Apostle Paul lays out the source of our strength clearly:

"For God has not given us a spirit of timidity, but of power and love and discipline" (2 Timothy 1:7, NASB).

The word translated here as "discipline" is the same word often translated as self-control.

This means that when you feel timid, panicked, or out of control, you can lean on the truth that God has already placed within you the Spirit of power, love, and discipline (self-control). You don't have to try to manufacture this strength on your own.

Self-control is primarily about managing the things you can control: your words, your reactions, your spending, and your focus. It means choosing a reasoned, faithful response over a raw, emotional one.

The Battlefield of Reaction

Self-control is often tested in the moments right after a stressful event related to your child.

Maybe you got a hurtful text, heard a piece of bad news, or had a difficult, manipulative conversation. Your heart starts racing, and your impulse is to react immediately — to send an angry reply, to call and argue, or to immediately share the bad news with everyone you know.

In these moments, you must learn to pause. That pause is the space where self-control works.

1. Control Your Words

Words are the sharpest weapon we possess, and in moments of crisis, they can do irreparable harm. When your child is being hurtful or demanding, self-control means refusing to sink to their level.

The book of Proverbs, which is full of practical wisdom, teaches us that controlling our tongue is the mark of a wise person: "In the abundance of words there is transgression, but the one who restrains his lips is wise" (Proverbs 10:19, NASB).

When your phone buzzes with an upsetting message, put it down.

Do not respond for at least an hour. Pray instead of typing. Self-control doesn't mean you don't feel anger; it means you choose to restrain your lips and wait until you can respond with love, not with fire.

2. Control Your Focus

As we discussed in the "Captive Thoughts" chapter, the mind is a battlefield. Self-control means directing your thoughts toward God's truth, rather than letting them run wild with catastrophic "what-ifs."

Self-control in your focus means deciding what information you will consume and when.

If checking social media for updates on your child brings you crushing anxiety, self-control means you choose to not look for a day or a week. You are putting a harness on your impulse to obsessively worry.

The philosopher Plato (428/427–348/347 BC) once wrote that the first and best victory is to conquer self: "The first and best victory is to conquer self; to be conquered by self is, of all things, the most shameful and vile." While he meant this philosophically, for the Christian, conquering the self means submitting our impulses to the Spirit of God.

Cultivating the Fruit

Self-control is listed as one of the nine "fruit of the Spirit": "But the fruit of the Spirit is love, joy, peace, patience, kindness, goodness, faithfulness, gentleness, self-control; against such things there is no law" (Galatians 5:22–23, NASB).

A fruit is something that grows slowly, over time, and requires cultivation.

You can't just wish for an apple; you have to plant the tree, water it, and patiently wait for it to mature. Here is how you cultivate the fruit of self-control during this season:

1. Plant the Seed of Consistency

Self-control grows best in the soil of consistent, small disciplines.

Start with small victories: consistently getting up at the same time, consistently spending ten minutes in prayer, or consistently avoiding one distracting habit (like checking your phone every five minutes).

Each small victory builds the muscle for the bigger battles.

2. Water with the Spirit

Since self-control is a fruit of the Spirit, you need to rely on the Spirit to grow it.

Every day, pray this simple prayer: "Holy Spirit, I feel out of control. I invite You to give me the power, love, and discipline I need today." Relying on the Spirit shifts the burden from your weak human willpower to God's endless power.

3. Seek Accountability

Self-control is strongest when it is supported by your community.

Ask your spouse or a trusted friend (your Accountability Partner from a previous chapter) to hold you accountable to your goals. You can say, "If I receive a difficult text from my child, I will not respond until I talk to you first." This simple commitment creates an external fence to guard your internal reaction.

When you consistently exercise self-control, you stop making impulsive, fear-driven decisions and start making wise, faith-filled responses. You are bringing order and calm back into the one space you truly possess: your own heart and mind. This is not only your path to peace, but the most stable foundation you can offer your child when they finally decide to look for home.

References

- 2 Timothy 1:7 (NASB)
- Proverbs 10:19 (NASB)
- Galatians 5:22–23 (NASB)

Historical and Anecdotal References:

Plato Quote: "The first and best victory is to conquer self; to be conquered by self is, of all things, the most shameful and vile." This highlights the classical view of self-mastery.

- *Reference: https://www.iep.utm.edu/plato/*

Reflection

Take a few minutes to reflect and meditate on what you just read. Write down your thoughts and take time to pray and praise God.

Day 14
Serving Others

Serving Others: The Outward Glance of Faith

When you are deeply focused on a huge problem—like the ongoing grief of a child walking away—it can feel like your world has shrunk down to just your pain.

Every thought, every conversation, and every ounce of your energy is dedicated to the one crisis.

While it is necessary to process your grief, getting stuck in this narrow focus is dangerous. If all you ever look at is the pain in your own life, you lose sight of the bigger picture: the desperate need of the world around you.

The antidote to being crushed by your own problems is the outward glance of faith—a deliberate choice to look past your own heartache and choose to serve someone else.

This chapter is about why serving others, especially those who can never pay you back, is one of the most powerful ways to heal and maintain spiritual perspective.

The Prescription for Self-Focus

Serving is a necessary discipline because it forces us out of the natural human tendency toward self-absorption. When you are serving, you are reminded that your pain, while real, is only one piece of the world's larger suffering.

The Bible provides a clear, strong command against living solely for our own needs and interests. The Apostle Paul urged the believers in Philippi to adopt a mindset that actively looks outward:

"Do nothing from selfishness or empty conceit, but with humility consider one another as more important than yourselves; do not merely look out for your own personal interests, but also for the interests of others" (Philippians 2:3-4, NASB).

When you are consumed by your own problem, you are violating this command—not out of malice, but out of a paralyzing grief.

By choosing to serve, you are exercising humility and obeying the direct command to look out for the interests of others.

The Unexpected Gift of Serving

It may seem counterintuitive, but when you spend time focusing on someone else's need, your own burden momentarily feels lighter. This is because serving shifts your energy from worry (which drains you) to purpose (which fills you).

The great humanitarian and Nobel Peace Prize winner Dr. Albert Schweitzer understood this principle perfectly.

He left a successful career in Europe to practice medicine in Africa, famously saying, "The only really happy people are those who have learned how to serve."

Dr. Schweitzer recognized that deep, lasting happiness isn't found by fixing your own life, but by dedicating it to something larger than yourself. When you serve, you step directly into God's purpose, and that purpose is always more fulfilling than any pain can be consuming.

Seeking the True Audience: Those Who Cannot Repay

The Bible is very specific about who we should prioritize serving: the vulnerable, the marginalized, and the poor. These are the people who offer no earthly return, which ensures your motive is pure—you are serving God, not man.

The book of James defines pure, true religion in a simple, practical way: "Pure and undefiled religion in the sight of our God and Father is this: to visit orphans and widows in their distress, and to keep oneself unstained by the world" (James 1:27, NASB).

Notice the action items:

- ✓ Visit orphans and widows: This represents serving those who are helpless and alone (the vulnerable).

- ✓ Keep oneself unstained by the world: This represents the necessity of guarding your spiritual focus (self-control).

For a Christian parent who is grieving, serving these groups provides a unique, spiritual balm:

It Replaces Self-Pity with Empathy:

When you spend time with a homeless person who has truly lost everything, your own situation—though painful—gains perspective. Your heart opens up to the suffering of others, which naturally shrinks the feeling of self-pity.

It Reminds You of God's Provision:

When you are the one giving a meal or offering comfort, you are reminded that God has blessed you so you can be a blessing. This shifts your focus from what you lack (the perfect family) to what you have (the ability to give).

It Honors God:

Jesus made it clear that when we serve the least, we are serving Him directly: "Truly I say to you, to the extent that you did it to one of these brothers of Mine, even the least of them, you did it to Me" (Matthew 25:40, NASB).

Practical Ways to Serve

You do not need to quit your job and move to another country to serve. You can weave this powerful discipline into your current life:

Find a Consistent Commitment:

Instead of doing a big, one-time project, commit to a small, regular action. Serve at a soup kitchen once a month, volunteer at a retirement home every Saturday morning, or commit to regularly assisting a single parent or elderly neighbor with yard work. Consistency is more important than size.

<u>Serve as a Family (or Couple):</u>

Serving together with your spouse or remaining children strengthens your Inner Circle. It gives you a shared, outward purpose that unites you and replaces time you might have otherwise spent worrying.

<u>Use Your Gifting:</u>

If you are a good organizer, organize a drive for the homeless shelter. If you are good at listening, volunteer to staff a non-crisis support line. Use the talents God has given you to meet someone else's need.

Serving others is the ultimate act of active faith. It proves that you trust God enough with your own chaotic situation to still be available for His mission. It is the outward glance that brings the inward healing. When you choose to pour out your life for others, God pours His peace back into you.

Debbie and I do several things together to serve others:

- We go on short term missions trips around the world
- We serve other couples who are hurting and in a similar situation as us
- We participate in other service opportunities at our local church

There really is a lot of power, peace and joy when you choose to serve others!

References

- Philippians 2:3–4 (NASB)
- James 1:27 (NASB)
- Matthew 25:40 (NASB)

Historical and Anecdotal References:

Dr. Albert Schweitzer Quote: "The only really happy people are those who have learned how to serve." This quote reflects the principle behind his decision to dedicate his life to humanitarian work.

- Reference: *https://www.schweitzerfellowship.org/aboutus/albert-schweitzer*

Reflection

Take a few minutes to reflect and meditate on what you just read. Write down your thoughts and take time to pray and praise God.

_____
_____
_____
_____
_____
_____
_____
_____
_____
_____
_____
_____
_____
_____
_____
_____
_____

Day 15

Empathy

Walking Alongside: The Power of Shared Pain

If you've been on this journey for any length of time, you know the truth: No one truly understands this specific kind of pain unless they've been there.

People can be kind and supportive, but only a parent whose adult child has walked away from family and faith knows the unique mix of grief, guilt, fear, and enduring hope that you carry every day.

Because this pain is so specific, finding and connecting with other parents who get it is not just helpful—it's essential for your emotional survival and your spiritual health.

This chapter is about moving beyond just knowing others share your struggle and actively choosing to show empathy and share strength with them.

The Difference Between Sympathy and Empathy

When you talk to someone who hasn't been through this, you usually get sympathy. Sympathy says, "I feel sorry for you, and I hope things get better." It's nice, but it creates a distance; it puts you in the role of the victim needing rescue.

What you need, and what you can give, is empathy. Empathy is different. Empathy says, "I know that deep, awful feeling in your gut, because I have it too. You are not alone." It's a shared experience that creates a powerful, supportive bridge.

The Bible calls us to this deep, shared connection: "Rejoice with those who rejoice, and weep with those who weep" (Romans 12:15, NASB).

When another parent is sharing their latest heartbreak with you, you don't need to offer advice or a quick fix. You just need to show up and weep with them or quietly sit with them.

This act of shared mourning is profound. It validates their pain, and in doing so, it validates your own. When you offer your understanding to someone else, you give yourself the permission to feel understood as well.

The Danger of Comparison (Again)

In an earlier chapter, we talked about the danger of envy and bitterness toward families whose children seem successful. But comparison is also a trap when dealing with families who share your pain.

It is tempting to listen to someone else's story and think: "Well, my child is only doing X; theirs is doing Y. Maybe my situation isn't that bad." Or conversely: "Their child is only gone for a month; mine has been gone for five years. My pain is worse."

This mental measuring game is spiritual quicksand! It destroys empathy and prevents true fellowship. Every parent's journey is a unique crisis, and God calls us to stand shoulder-to-shoulder, not to stack our traumas against each other.

The Apostle Paul reminds us that we all rely on the same grace regardless of the size or severity of our specific trouble: "God is faithful, who will not allow you to be tempted beyond what you are able, but with the temptation will provide the way of escape also, so that you will be able to endure it" (1 Corinthians 10:13, NASB).

God gives you and your friend the strength to endure your specific trial. We are all equal at the foot of the cross, and we are all equal in the struggle for enduring faith. Focus on their pain, not on comparing the details.

The Practical Power of Shared Experience

When you connect with another parent who truly understands, several important things happen that promote healing:

1. You Get Permission to be Honest

In a support setting, you don't have to use spiritual platitudes or pretend you have it all together. You can say, "I am terrified," or "I am angry at God," or "I feel like a total failure." Hearing another Christian parent admit to the same raw, ugly feelings gives you the freedom to be honest with yourself and with God.

2. You Share Practical Wisdom

Another parent who has walked this road ahead of you can offer priceless wisdom that a pastor or counselor cannot. They know the emotional landmines—when to back off, when to send a simple text, or how to handle holidays. They help you with the small, difficult decisions that accumulate stress.

3. You become a Source of Hope

When you reach out to a newer parent in crisis, you become a powerful, living testimony of endurance. By sharing your story of how you survived the first year, or how God brought you through a specific dark moment, you offer a tangible, real-life hope that is often stronger than any abstract sermon.

The great physicist and humanitarian Albert Einstein noted, "Our task must be to free ourselves by widening our circle of compassion to embrace all living creatures and the whole of nature in its beauty."

For us, this means widening our circle of compassion to embrace the pain of others, especially those who share our specific burden.

Where to Find and Offer Empathy

You don't have to wait for someone to come to you. You can intentionally seek out and create spaces for shared empathy:

<u>Church-Based Support Groups:</u>

Many churches offer groups specifically for parents of prodigals (wayward children). These groups are invaluable because they combine shared pain with biblical teaching.

Mentoring:

If you are a few years into this journey, find a parent who is just starting out and offer them your quiet strength. This is the best way to turn your pain into purpose.

Prayer Partnerships:

Commit to praying regularly with one other parent who shares your burden. When your strength fails, theirs will cover you, and vice versa.

The pain you are carrying is real, but it doesn't have to be isolating.

By actively reaching out and offering your empathy to others, you honor your own experience and gain the deep, sustaining comfort of knowing you are part of a brave, enduring family of faith.

References

- Romans 12:15 (NASB)
- 1 Corinthians 10:13 (NASB)

Historical and Anecdotal References:

Albert Einstein Quote: "Our task must be to free ourselves by widening our circle of compassion..." This highlights the profound value of extending empathy to others.

- o   *Reference: https://www.einstein-website.de/zitate/zitate_en.html*

Reflection

Take a few minutes to reflect and meditate on what you just read. Write down your thoughts and take time to pray and praise God.

Day 16

Vulnerability

The Strength of Being Seen: Choosing Vulnerability

In all the previous chapters, we've talked about finding peace, setting boundaries, enduring hardship, and connecting with others. All of that requires one courageous choice: vulnerability.

Vulnerability is simply the willingness to be seen—to let others know that you are hurting, that you don't have all the answers, and that your life is not perfect.

When your adult child is walking a difficult path, the natural instinct is to hide that pain. We fear that if we share our struggle, we will be judged as bad parents, or that our faith will look weak.

But the Christian life is not about pretending we are strong.

It's about relying on a God who is strong, especially in our weakness. Choosing to be vulnerable isn't an act of weakness; it's one of the bravest, most healing acts of faith you can perform.

The Myth of the Perfect Parent

Many Christian parents carry the heavy weight of the "Perfect Parent Myth." This lie tells us that if we were truly faithful, our children would never stray. When they do, we feel compelled to hide the situation to protect our reputation, which leads to spiritual isolation.

This kind of fear-based hiding is a direct block to the grace God wants to give you through others. The Bible encourages honesty about our shortcomings and our need for help.

The Apostle James links confession and vulnerability directly to healing: "Therefore, confess your sins to one another, and pray for one another, so that you may be healed. The effective prayer of a righteous man can accomplish much" (James 5:16, NASB).

While the verse speaks of confessing sin, the principle applies to confessing our needs, fears, and brokenness. When you are vulnerable with a trusted brother or sister in Christ, you give them the opportunity to pray for you—and their "effective prayer" can accomplish much in your life and in the life of your child.

Vulnerability as a Shared Burden

Think about the story of the four friends who wanted to bring their paralyzed friend to Jesus. The crowd was so thick that they couldn't get through the door. What did they do? They climbed onto the roof, tore a hole in it, and lowered their friend down into the room where Jesus was (Luke 5:17–26).

This dramatic action required great vulnerability.

The man had to be seen in his helpless state by everyone. His friends had to publicly expose their desperate need for Jesus. When you are vulnerable and share your pain, you are essentially doing the same thing: You are allowing others to help lower you and your child into the presence of Jesus through prayer and support. You cannot climb onto the roof alone.

The Three Fears that Block Vulnerability

What stops us from being honest? Usually, it's one of three deep fears. Recognizing them is the first step toward overcoming them:

1. The Fear of Judgment ("They will blame me.")

This fear is powerful. We worry that people will analyze our parenting techniques, our church attendance, or our past mistakes. But genuine Christian community, led by the Spirit, is defined by grace, not condemnation.

When you choose to open up, you model grace. You give others permission to look past your performance and see your human heart. You are saying, "Yes, I made mistakes, but God is still faithful."

2. The Fear of Hopelessness ("I don't have the answers.")

We often feel we need to present a plan or an update on our child's progress. But vulnerability means saying, "I have no idea what tomorrow holds, and I don't know why this is happening."

The great missionary and author Amy Carmichael (1867–1951), who dedicated her life to rescuing children in India, lived a life filled with hardship and unanswered prayers.

She understood that sometimes, we simply have to rely on a quiet trust. She famously said, "If I stoop, it is to listen." When you are vulnerable, you stoop to listen to God and to those around you, admitting that your own understanding is too limited to guide you.

3. The Fear of Permanence ("I'll be stuck in this story.")

You might fear that once you tell people about your pain, that crisis will become your permanent identity — that every time someone sees you, they will only see "the parent with the prodigal."

The answer to this is found in controlling the narrative. When you are vulnerable, make sure you share not just the pain, but also the faithfulness of God in the middle of the pain. Your story isn't just about your child's choices; it is about your God's enduring love.

How to Practice Openness

Vulnerability is a process, not a sudden leap. Here are steps to start practicing it today:

Start Small (The Inner Circle):

Begin by being completely honest with your spouse, a prayer partner, or one trusted, seasoned friend (your Confidante). Practice saying the raw, true sentence out loud: "I feel like a failure right now."

Use "I" Statements: Share your feelings and fears without making accusations or revealing unnecessary details about your child. Example: Instead of saying, "My child is doing something terrible," say, "I am struggling with fear over my child's future."

Share the Good News:

When God answers a small prayer or gives you a moment of peace, share that too! Vulnerability means sharing both the struggle and the faithfulness. This encourages the person listening and reminds you that the story is still being written by God.

Your willingness to be vulnerable with your spiritual family is the most powerful weapon against the isolation that grief creates. It is the final, essential step in moving from merely surviving your pain to finding healing and purpose in the community of Christ.

References

- James 5:16 (NASB)
- Luke 5:17–26 (The anecdote of the paralyzed man)

Historical and Anecdotal References:

Amy Carmichael Quote: "If I stoop, it is to listen." The quote emphasizes humility, quiet attention, and a life surrendered to God's purpose, often through deep suffering.

- o *Reference: https://www.dohnavur.com/amy-carmichael-quotes/*

Paul Beersdorf

Reflection

Take a few minutes to reflect and meditate on what you just read. Write down your thoughts and take time to pray and praise God.

Day 17

Influence vs. Control

Influence, Not Control: The Freedom of Letting Go

For Christian parents in your situation, the feeling of loss of control is one of the heaviest burdens. You poured your life into raising your child, only to watch them make choices you can't change, fix, or stop.

This loss of control often leads to emotional panic, where you try to force an outcome.

You might try to persuade, argue, manipulate, or financially pressure your adult child, all because you desperately want to regain the control you once had when they were young.

But here is the essential spiritual truth: You cannot control another person, and God never asked you to. God gave you the power to influence and to love, but the power of control belongs to Him alone. Recognizing and accepting the difference between these two things is the key to finding peace in this journey.

Defining the Line: Influence vs. Control

It is vital to understand what your role is and what God's role is.

<u>1. Control (God's Role)</u>

Control is the power to dictate, command, and guarantee an outcome. Control demands immediate results and seeks power over another person's free will. When we try to control our children, we are stepping outside of our lane and trying to play God. This always leads to frustration, resentment, and a damaged relationship.

2. Influence (Your Role)

Influence is the power to affect, shape, guide, and inspire through example, prayer, and persistent love. Influence respects the free will of the other person and focuses entirely on the actions you take. Your primary tools of influence are your prayers and your peaceful, Christ-like life.

We see the line between control and influence drawn clearly by Jesus. He never forced anyone to follow Him. He said, "If anyone wishes to come after Me, he must deny himself, and take up his cross daily and follow Me" (Luke 9:23, NASB).

The choice to follow is always up to the individual. If Jesus respected human free will and refused to control people, how can we, as mere parents, think we have the right to force our adult children to submit to our will?

The Dangers of Trying to Control

When we try to control our adult child, we actually push them further away. Control tactics trigger resentment and rebellion, especially in an adult who is fiercely guarding their independence.

Some common tactics of control include:

Emotional Manipulation: Using guilt, tears, or threats of withdrawal to force compliance.

Financial Leverage: Using money or assistance as a reward for making "right" choices.

Constant Preaching/Arguing: Engaging in endless debates to try to logically convince them to change their mind.

These attempts at control come from a place of fear, but they communicate a message of distrust to your child.

They hear, "I don't trust God to work, so I have to do it myself," and "I don't trust you to make good choices." This is why control is ultimately the opposite of biblical love, which "does not seek its own" (1 Corinthians 13:5, NASB).

The famous English author C.S. Lewis, who wrote extensively about free will and temptation, recognized that even God will not violate the freedom of choice. He stated: "God created things which had free will. That meant creatures which can go wrong or right."

If God honors the free will of His children, even knowing the pain and mistakes that will come from it, then we must align our parenting—even with adult children—to honor that same, often painful, freedom.

The Power of True Influence

When you let go of the impossible task of control, you are free to pick up the powerful task of influence. Your influence is rooted in two indestructible sources:

1. The Influence of Prayer

Your most powerful act of influence is not your words to your child, but your prayers to God for your child.

Prayer is the one way you can genuinely affect your child's life without violating their free will. When you pray, you invite the Holy Spirit—the ultimate influence—to work in ways you cannot see or imagine.

The Apostle Paul gives us the perfect framework for this kind of persistent, hope-filled influence: "We have confidence in the Lord concerning you, that you are doing and will continue to do what we command. May the Lord direct your hearts into the love of God and into the steadfastness of Christ" (2 Thessalonians 3:4–5, NASB).

When you pray, you are asking the Lord to direct your child's heart. You are not demanding the destination; you are asking the ultimate Guide to influence their direction. This is active influence, and it is a work of patience and deep faith.

2. The Influence of Peace

The most magnetic force you possess is the peace you carry, regardless of your child's decisions. When your child sees you living a stable, joyful, and purposeful life—continuing your work, serving others, and maintaining fellowship—they witness a living demonstration of the power of the Gospel.

When your child finally hits a wall and is looking for an anchor, they will not be drawn back by a parent who is panicking and trying to control them. They will be drawn to the parent who is peaceful, firm in faith, and unconditionally loving.

Your peace, which we discussed in an earlier chapter, becomes a quiet, steady beacon of hope. It tells them: "My faith is real enough to withstand your choices, and God is faithful enough to remain good even when things look bad."

Release the need to control. Embrace the power of influence through prayer and your faithful example. When you let go of what you cannot change, you find the freedom to truly love the person God created your child to be.

References

- Luke 9:23 (NASB)
- 1 Corinthians 13:5 (NASB)
- 2 Thessalonians 3:4–5 (NASB)

Historical and Anecdotal References:

C.S. Lewis Quote: "God created things which had free will. That meant creatures which can go wrong or right." This reflects the theological concept of free will, a key element in Lewis's writings.

- *Reference: https://www.cslewis.com/*

Reflection

Take a few minutes to reflect and meditate on what you just read. Write down your thoughts and take time to pray and praise God.

Day 18

God's Promises

Holding the Promises: The Unshakeable Foundation

If you have walked through the previous chapters, you've learned to pray, set boundaries, seek counsel, and conquer bitterness. You've done the hard work of enduring. But on the days when the grief still feels overwhelming, or the fear seems to win the battle for your mind, where do you go?

You must go to the promises of God.

A promise from God is not a hopeful maybe; it is a guarantee. It is the one thing in your entire life that you can place your full weight on without fear of it collapsing. When the ground is shaking beneath you — when your family looks broken and your future looks uncertain — God's promises are the unshakeable foundation that keeps you standing.

This chapter is about learning to lean into the specific promises of God, using them as your strength and your shield during this difficult season.

The Nature of God's Word

In a world full of broken contracts and failed commitments, we often view God's promises through a skeptical, human lens. We think, "Maybe that promise applies to someone else, or maybe it only applied back then." This is a huge mistake.

The Bible tells us that God cannot lie, and His promises are eternal. The Psalmist wrote: "Forever, O Lord, Your word is firmly fixed in heaven" (Psalm 119:89, NASB).

When we read a promise in the Bible, it is a truth that is "firmly fixed"—it is settled, unchanging, and totally reliable. This means that your hope is not based on your child's next decision, or on your latest prayer performance, but on the character of the God who made the promise.

Promise vs. Prediction

It's crucial to understand that leaning into a promise is not the same as demanding a specific prediction. God has not promised that your child will return on a Tuesday morning at 10 a.m.

Instead, He has promised things about His own character that are true no matter what your child does:

He is faithful (He keeps His word).

He is sovereign (He is ultimately in control).

He is good (He works all things for the good of those who love Him).

When you choose to believe these overarching promises, the smaller details of your child's life lose their power to completely overwhelm you.

The Promises to Claim in the Wilderness

When you are praying for a wayward child, there are three categories of promises you must claim and repeat every single day.

<u>1. The Promise of God's Unwavering Presence</u>

The deepest fear of a grieving parent is that they are walking this road alone. God's Word promises the opposite. He is not a distant, hands-off Father; He is intimately present in your deepest pain.

Claim this Promise: "Be strong and courageous, do not be afraid or tremble at them, for the Lord your God is the one who goes with you. He will not fail you or forsake you" (Deuteronomy 31:6, NASB).

You can speak this promise directly to your fear: "Lord, I am afraid of tomorrow, but Your Word says You will not fail me or forsake me." This promise gives you the courage to wake up and face another day, knowing you are never truly alone.

2. The Promise of God's Purpose in Pain

It's easy to feel that the pain you are enduring is wasted — that this whole situation is a failure with no purpose. But God has promised that He wastes nothing; He uses every moment of suffering to create something beautiful in you and through you.

Claim this Promise: "And we know that God causes all things to work together for good to those who love God, to those who are called according to His purpose" (Romans 8:28, NASB).

This promise is an anchor. It doesn't say "all things are good," but that God causes all things to "work together for good."

This means that even the hurtful phone calls, the painful anniversaries, and the years of separation are being woven by a divine hand into a pattern of goodness and ultimate redemption. This promise gives your pain purpose, preventing it from becoming pure despair.

3. The Promise of Answered Prayer (in His Will)

When we pray for our child, we often doubt that God is listening or cares. The promise is not that we get exactly what we demand, but that when we pray in alignment with His heart, He hears and acts.

Claim this Promise: "And this is the confidence which we have before Him, that, if we ask anything according to His will, He hears us. And if we know that He hears us in whatever we ask, we know that we have the requests which we have asked from Him" (1 John 5:14-15, NASB).

It is always God's will for your child to be saved, loved, and redeemed.

Therefore, when you pray for your child's spiritual salvation and restoration, you are praying "according to His will." This promise assures you that God not only hears you but is actively working toward that redemptive goal, even if His timeline is different from yours.

The Legacy of Enduring Faith

The ability to cling to God's promises in the face of contradictory evidence is the very definition of faith. The writer of Hebrews reminds us that the great heroes of faith all lived and died without seeing the full completion of God's promises in their lifetime:

"All these died in faith, without receiving the promises, but having seen them and having welcomed them from a distance, and having confessed that they were strangers and exiles on the earth" (Hebrews 11:13, NASB).

Even those ancient heroes had to hold onto the promise "from a distance." Your task is the same. You may not see the end of your child's story today, but you hold onto the promises of a faithful God.

The great reformer Martin Luther (1483-1546), who faced immense persecution and turmoil, summarized the power of a promise-based faith: "I have held many things in my hands, and I have lost them all; but whatever I have placed in God's hands, that I still possess."

Parent, you have placed the heaviest burden—your child and their eternal future—into God's hands. Now, you must choose to let the promises of God hold you. Let them be the unshakeable truth that defines your hope and your peace, regardless of what tomorrow may bring.

References

- Psalm 119:89 (NASB)
- Deuteronomy 31:6 (NASB)
- Romans 8:28 (NASB)
- 1 John 5:14-15 (NASB)
- Luke 9:23 (NASB)
- 1 Corinthians 13:5 (NASB)
- 2 Thessalonians 3:4-5 (NASB)
- Hebrews 11:13 (NASB)

Historical and Anecdotal References:

Martin Luther Quote: "I have held many things in my hands..." This quote emphasizes the security of a faith placed in God.

- Reference: https://www.luther.de/en/

Reflection

Take a few minutes to reflect and meditate on what you just read. Write down your thoughts and take time to pray and praise God.

_____
_____
_____
_____
_____
_____
_____
_____
_____
_____
_____
_____
_____
_____
_____
_____
_____
_____

Day 19
God's Comfort

Finding Rest: The Arms of God's Comfort

If you've read this far, you are a parent who is weary but not defeated. You are a parent who has faced the wilderness, set boundaries, fought toxic thoughts, and clung fiercely to the promises of God.

But even the most enduring hearts need rest.

The spiritual marathon you are running requires regular moments where you simply stop striving, stop worrying, and allow yourself to be held by the only One who fully understands your pain. This chapter is about leaving the battlefield for a moment and finding true, deep rest in the arms of God's comfort.

The God of All Comfort

It is essential to know the biblical name for the source of your peace: He is the "God of all comfort."

The Apostle Paul wrote this incredible truth to believers who were facing persecution and hardship, a suffering that was very real and very painful:

"Blessed be the God and Father of our Lord Jesus Christ, the Father of mercies and God of all comfort, who comforts us in all our affliction so that we will be able to comfort those who are in any affliction with the comfort with which we ourselves are comforted by God" (2 Corinthians 1:3-4, NASB).

Notice the beautiful flow of this promise:

God's Identity: He is the "God of all comfort" and the "Father of mercies." His nature is tender, gentle, and overflowing with compassion.

God's Action: He comforts "us in all our affliction." There is no grief, fear, or heartache related to your child that is too small or too large for His comfort.

God's Purpose: He comforts you so that you can then "comfort those who are in any affliction." Your pain is not just for you; it is being prepared for a future purpose—to show empathy to another parent who will one day stand where you stand.

You are being comforted so that you can comfort. That purpose prevents your pain from becoming pointless.

The Barrier of Guilt

One of the biggest obstacles to receiving God's comfort is guilt. You might feel like you don't deserve comfort because you failed as a parent, or because you still get angry sometimes, or because you haven't been as faithful as you should be.

Guilt keeps you at an arm's length from God, making you feel like you have to clean yourself up before you can approach Him. But this misunderstanding strips God of His role as the Father of mercies.

The prophet Isaiah gave us the tender image of a gentle, comforting shepherd: "Like a shepherd He will tend His flock, in His arm He will gather the lambs and carry them in the fold of His robe; He will gently lead the nursing ewes" (Isaiah 40:11, NASB).

When you feel wounded, exhausted, or weak, you are the lamb He gathers into His arms. When you feel drained, you are the nursing ewe He gently leads. You don't have to be strong to come to Him; you must be weak. All you have to do is surrender your pride and let yourself be carried.

The great Christian thinker Saint Augustine (354–430 AD) understood that our deepest restlessness prevents us from receiving this rest. He famously prayed, "You have made us for Yourself, O Lord, and our hearts are restless until they find their rest in You."

Your heart's restlessness over your child can only be calmed when you choose to find your rest, your security, and your identity in God, not in the state of your family.

How to Receive Comfort

Comfort is a gift you must actively receive. It requires intentional steps to stop the striving and simply be still.

1. Give Him Your Tears

You do not have to put on a brave face for God. Your grief is not too messy for Him. The Psalms—the prayer book of the Bible—are full of people crying out in despair, anger, and confusion.

The Psalmist trusted God so much that he asked God to literally record his tears: "You have taken account of my wanderings; Put my tears in Your bottle. Are they not in Your book?" (Psalm 56:8, NASB).

When you are alone, allow yourself to cry and tell God exactly how much this hurts. Let Him collect your tears. This surrender of emotion is a powerful first step toward receiving peace.

2. Practice Stillness

In a life dominated by worry, stillness is hard, but it is the prerequisite for peace. As we saw earlier, God commanded His people, "Be still, and know that I am God; I will be exalted among the nations, I will be exalted in the earth" (Psalm 46:10, NASB).

Self-control is doing the right thing; stillness is resting in the right Person. Set aside five minutes today where you do nothing but breathe slowly and repeat one simple phrase: "I am still. You are God." In that quiet moment, you exchange your burden for His presence.

3. Embrace the Great Exchange

The ultimate comfort we have is that Jesus willingly took all our pain, sorrow, and sin so that we could have His peace. This is the great exchange.

The prophet Isaiah foretold this exchange: "He was despised and forsaken of men, a man of sorrows and acquainted with grief… But He was pierced for our offenses, He was crushed for our iniquities; the chastisement for our well-being fell upon Him, and by His wounds we are healed" (Isaiah 53:3, 5, NASB).

When you feel the weight of parental guilt or the crushing pressure of grief, remember that Jesus was "acquainted with grief" too. He bore your sorrow on the cross so that the "chastisement for your well-being" (or peace) could fall upon Him.

You do not have to carry this grief anymore.

Lay it at the foot of the cross, close your eyes, and allow the God of all comfort to finally give you rest. Your journey of enduring faith is beautiful, but every enduring warrior must take time to heal and rest in the embrace of their Father.

References

- 2 Corinthians 1:3-4 (NASB)
- Isaiah 40:11 (NASB)
- Psalm 56:8 (NASB)
- Psalm 46:10 (NASB)
- Isaiah 53:3, 5 (NASB)

Historical and Anecdotal References:

Saint Augustine Quote: "You have made us for Yourself, O Lord, and our hearts are restless until they find their rest in You," from his Confessions.

- *Reference: https://www.ccel.org/ccel/augustine/confessions.iv.html*

Reflection

Take a few minutes to reflect and meditate on what you just read. Write down your thoughts and take time to pray and praise God.

_____
_____
_____
_____
_____
_____
_____
_____
_____
_____
_____
_____
_____
_____
_____
_____
_____
_____
_____
_____

Day 20

Trusting God

Surrender and Total Trust

You have spent many chapters learning how to fight—how to fight the battle for your mind, how to fight the urge to compromise, and how to fight the temptation to isolate. But there comes a point in every spiritual battle where the greatest act of faith is not fighting harder, but surrendering completely.

Surrender, in the context of your wayward child, is not giving up on your child; it is giving up control of the outcome to God.

It is the deep, quiet, definitive decision to say: "Lord, I have done all I can do. I trust You with the next chapter, even if that chapter is painful. I choose to rest in Your sovereignty."

This act of total trust is the only thing that will fully lift the crushing weight of responsibility from your shoulders.

The Weight of the Unshared Burden

When you don't surrender, you are operating under a terrible illusion: that you are the primary savior in your child's life. You may not consciously think it, but every moment of obsessive worry, every attempt to fix, and every sleepless night is proof that you have kept the burden entirely on yourself.

The Bible gives us a simple, clear command for handling the burdens that are too heavy for us to carry:

"Therefore humble yourselves under the mighty hand of God, that He may exalt you at the proper time, casting all your anxiety on Him, because He cares for you" (1 Peter 5:6–7, NASB).

Notice the link: You humble yourself (surrender your control) and cast your anxiety (your burden) on Him. The Greek word for "casting" means to literally "hurl" or "throw" the weight off your back and onto something else.

You are commanded to hurl the anxiety over your child onto God because He is mighty enough to hold it, and because He cares for you. You are not throwing the burden onto a busy God who might drop it; you are casting it onto a Father whose very nature is to care.

What Surrender Is Not

To truly surrender, you must first clear up the common misunderstandings about what it means:

Surrender is NOT apathy.

It is not saying, "I don't care anymore." It is saying, "I care so much that I am willing to trust the only One who can truly help."

Surrender is NOT stopping prayer.

It is changing your prayer from "My will be done" (e.g., "Bring them home now") to "Your will be done" (e.g., "Do Your redemptive work in their life, however and whenever You see fit").

Surrender is NOT ceasing influence.

As we discussed, you are still called to love, pray, and model Christ. Surrender means you do those things without fear, because the outcome is no longer your job.

The great Christian missionary and martyr Jim Elliot (1927–1956) powerfully understood the distinction between human desire and divine purpose when he said, "He is no fool who gives what he cannot keep to gain what he cannot lose."

When you surrender your child to God, you are giving Him the control (which you cannot keep anyway) to gain peace (which you cannot lose in Christ). You trade the illusion of control for the reality of God's power.

The Mechanics of Trust

Surrender is not a one-time decision; it is a daily practice of placing your child into the mighty hand of God. This practice requires a renewed confidence in three non-negotiable truths about God.

1. Trusting His Sovereignty (His Control)

Sovereignty means that God is the supreme authority, and nothing happens outside of His knowledge or allowance. This can be hard to swallow when facing painful choices, but it is the only true source of comfort.

Claim this Promise: "The Lord has established His throne in the heavens, and His sovereignty rules over all" (Psalm 103:19, NASB).

You trust that even the chaos, the rebellion, and the pain your child is experiencing are ultimately known to and ruled by a God who is working a master plan.

Your trust in His sovereignty allows you to stop trying to manage the universe and simply rest in the truth that He already is.

2. Trusting His Love (His Goodness)

We worry that if we fully surrender, God might "punish" our child or not love them as much as we do.

This is a profound insult to His character. God loves your child with a perfect, eternal, self-sacrificial love that you cannot possibly match.

Claim this Promise: "But God demonstrates His own love toward us, in that while we were still sinners, Christ died for us" (Romans 5:8, NASB).

If God demonstrated His love for us when we were His enemies, how much more does He actively love your child, whom He created and pursues?

Surrender means trusting that the heart caring for your child is infinitely more loving and more motivated toward redemption than yours is.

3. Trusting His Timeline (His Patience)

Our greatest challenge with surrender is patience. We want the fix now. But God's redemptive work often takes years, or even decades, as He allows consequences, suffering, and brokenness to guide a wayward heart back to Him.

Claim this Promise: "The Lord is not slow about His promise, as some count slowness, but is patient toward you, not wishing for any to perish, but for all to come to repentance" (2 Peter 3:9, NASB).

When you see slowness, God sees patience. He is patient with your child, giving them the maximum time and opportunity to come to repentance.

When you surrender your timeline to His, you are joining Him in that patient waiting, trusting that His desire for your child's salvation is far greater than your desire for immediate comfort.

Surrender, parent, and know the freedom of living under the mighty hand of God. The weight of worry is too heavy for you, but it is nothing to Him. Hurl it onto Him, and walk forward in the peace that comes from total trust.

References

- 1 Peter 5:6–7 (NASB)
- Luke 9:23 (NASB)
- 1 Corinthians 13:5 (NASB)
- Psalm 103:19 (NASB)
- Romans 5:8 (NASB)
- 2 Peter 3:9 (NASB)

Historical and Anecdotal References:

Jim Elliot Quote: "He is no fool who gives what he cannot keep to gain what he cannot lose." This quote emphasizes the eternal perspective required for true surrender.

- *Reference: https://www.wheaton.edu/academics/special-collections/collections/billy-graham-center-archives/jim-elliot/*

Reflection

Take a few minutes to reflect and meditate on what you just read. Write down your thoughts and take time to pray and praise God.

Day 21

Hope

Hope for the Future: The Certainty of God's Redemption

You are nearing the end of this journey through this devotional. You have learned how to endure, how to discipline your mind, and how to surrender your deepest burden. Now, as you look ahead, you must anchor your tired heart not just in the struggles of today, but in the certainty of God's future.

When you pray for your wayward adult child, you are often praying for what seems impossible—a complete reversal, a deep change of heart, and a full, lasting return to faith. Humanly speaking, this can feel like a fantasy. But for the Christian, hope is not wishful thinking; hope is absolute confidence in God's promises.

This chapter is about closing the book on your worry and opening your eyes to the powerful, redemptive work that God guarantees, both in this life and in the life to come.

The Definition of True Hope

In the world, hope means "I wish." In the Bible, hope means "I know for sure."

Biblical hope is not uncertain; it is the absolute assurance of things not yet seen. The writer of Hebrews gives us the defining verse of this confidence: "Now faith is the assurance of things hoped for, the conviction of things not seen" (Hebrews 11:1, NASB).

When you pray for your child, your hope is rooted in two unshakeable truths that God has promised:

Redemption is God's Nature: God's entire story, from Genesis to Revelation, is a story of taking what is broken—sinful people, failed situations, and deep suffering—and turning it into something beautiful, redemptive, and glorious.

God's Love is Persistent: Your child may run far and fast, but they can never outrun God's relentless, pursuing love. God's desire is for all to come to repentance (2 Peter 3:9), and He will pursue your child with a love that is more patient and more powerful than any distance your child has created.

This hope allows you to release the crippling fear that your child's story is already finished. You know that while there is breath, there is the potential for God's incredible intervention.

The Power of a Single Spark

Throughout history, God has demonstrated His power to change lives in an instant, often after years of wandering. Your child's story is never too complicated, too messy, or too far gone for Him.

Think of Augustine of Hippo (354-430 AD). He was one of the most influential theologians in Christian history, but for years, he lived a wild, pleasure-seeking life that broke his mother's heart. His mother, Monica, prayed for him relentlessly—for over seventeen years. She cried, she grieved, and she sought counsel, only to be told by a bishop, "It is impossible that the son of those tears should perish."

Monica did not give up her hope, even when all the evidence pointed to Augustine's destruction. Her relentless prayers were eventually answered in a dramatic conversion that led Augustine to become one of the greatest pillars of the Christian faith.

Monica's story is a powerful reminder that the length of the journey is not up to you; the persistence of your faith is. Your tears and your prayers are not wasted; they are part of a divine process. God is honoring your faithfulness, even when He hasn't yet revealed the final outcome.

The Ultimate Redemptive Guarantee

Your ultimate hope is not just for your child, but for the day when Christ returns and makes everything new. That future promise frames all our present pain.

The Apostle John wrote about a future where all the sorrow, worry, and brokenness you feel today will be completely wiped away:

"And I heard a loud voice from the throne, saying, 'Behold, the tabernacle of God is among men, and He will dwell among them, and they shall be His people, and God Himself will be among them, and He will wipe away every tear from their eyes; and there will no longer be any death; there will no longer be any mourning, or crying, or pain; for the first things have passed away'" (Revelation 21:3-4, NASB).

This is the guarantee that sustains you:

He will wipe away every tear: Every moment of grief, every sleepless night, every ounce of shame you have carried will be personally and permanently removed by God.

No more mourning, crying, or pain: The entire source of your current pain—your child's wandering, the broken relationship, the fear—will be gone. The "first things have passed away."

Holding onto this future promise allows you to live in the present with courage. Your earthly story with your child may be full of tribulation, but the heavenly story ends with absolute, guaranteed redemption and restoration.

Closing the Book, Running the Race

This devotional book is near the end, but your book of endurance continues. You have the tools, you have the community, and you have the promises.

As you step forward, remember the words of the great Christian hymn writer and abolitionist William Cowper (1731-1800). Cowper dealt with severe personal pain and mental illness, yet his faith remained a light: "God moves in a mysterious way His wonders to perform; He plants His footsteps in the sea, and rides upon the storm."

Your child's wandering is part of a mysterious way that God is still moving. He is in the storm; He is not absent.

Your job now is simple: Do not grow weary.

"Let us not lose heart in doing good, for in due time we will reap if we do not grow weary" (Galatians 6:9, NASB).

Do not grow weary in prayer. Do not grow weary in loving your child without compromising your truth. Do not grow weary in seeking fellowship and serving others. Trust in the God of all comfort, cling to His promises, and live today in the certainty of His glorious, future redemption.

Your hope is secure. Amen.

References

- Hebrews 11:1 (NASB)
- 2 Peter 3:9 (Implied)
- Revelation 21:3-4 (NASB)
- Galatians 6:9 (NASB)

Historical and Anecdotal References:

Saint Monica and Augustine of Hippo: Monica's 17 years of persistent prayer for her son, Augustine, is a classical model of enduring hope for a prodigal.

- *Reference: https://www.britannica.com/biography/Saint-Monica*

William Cowper Quote: "God moves in a mysterious way..." This quote reflects the enduring faith of a person who struggled deeply with mental and spiritual pain.

- *Reference: https://www.christianitytoday.com/history/issues/issue-28/william-cowper.html*

Reflection

Take a few minutes to reflect and meditate on what you just read. Write down your thoughts and take time to pray and praise God.

Day 22

When the answer is no

When the Answer is "No": Wrestling with God

You have prayed. You have begged. You have fasted. You have done everything you know to do as a faithful Christian parent.

Yet, the situation with your child remains unchanged, or perhaps even gets worse. The silence from heaven is deafening, and you look up and ask the toughest, most honest question of all: "Why, God? Why haven't You answered my prayer to save my child?"

This is the moment of crisis for your faith. The Wrestling with God chapter is where you confront the temptation to believe that God is either unwilling (He doesn't care about your pain) or unable (He's not powerful enough to change your child's heart). To find peace and endurance, you must choose honest wrestling with God instead of silent resentment or bitter retreat.

The Necessity of Honest Wrestling

Many Christians are taught that strong faith is quiet acceptance. The Bible shows us otherwise. Faith is an active, often painful, relationship that includes intense, honest wrestling. God is big enough for your doubts and your anger.

The Psalms—the very prayer book of the Bible—are full of people pushing back, arguing, and questioning God:

"How long, O Lord? Will You forget me forever? How long will You hide Your face from me?" (Psalm 13:1, NASB).

"Why do you stand far away, O Lord? Why do You hide Yourself in times of trouble?" (Psalm 10:1, NASB).

This wrestling is healthy because it brings your raw, unfiltered pain into the direct presence of God.

It is far better to wrestle with God in a fierce, open prayer than to shut down and resent Him in a quiet, resentful silence. Wrestling is an act of courageous trust—you are trusting that God loves you enough not to strike you down for being honest.

The Problem of "The Wrong Answer"

The pain of a "no" or a delayed answer stems from a crucial human misunderstanding: We confuse God's delay with God's indifference. We assume that if the answer isn't immediate and exactly what we asked for, God must not care about our situation.

The truth is, when you pray for your child's immediate return, you are asking for a surface-level fix to ease your pain. God, however, is likely working a deeper, slower work in the soul of your child—and in your own soul. He may be:

Allowing Consequences: Permitting your child to face the painful reality of their choices, which is often the sharpest tool the Holy Spirit uses to bring them to a place of desperation and repentance (think of the prodigal son).

Perfecting Your Weakness: Using the situation to grow profound character, patience, and unwavering faith in you.

The Apostle Paul spoke of his own unanswered prayer—his "thorn in the flesh"—and the profound answer God gave him:

"And He has said to me, 'My grace is sufficient for you, for power is perfected in weakness.' Most gladly, therefore, I will rather boast about my weaknesses, so that the power of Christ may dwell in me" (2 Corinthians 12:9, NASB).

God's answer to Paul's desperate prayer was not removal of the problem, but the perfection of power in weakness. When God seems to be saying "no" or "wait" to your specific request, He is giving you His grace, which is sufficient, and perfecting His power in your patient endurance.

The Certainty of God's Focused Attention

When the world feels chaotic and your prayers feel lost, you must surrender your limited understanding to God's perfect, mysterious will. You must trust that He can manage the vastness of creation while still caring for the individual needs of your family.

The famous astronomer Galileo Galilei spoke of the magnificent order of the universe and its Creator's focused attention, noting:

"The sun, with all those planets revolving around it and dependent on it, can still ripen a bunch of grapes as if it had nothing else in the universe to do."

If the physical universe, with billions of celestial bodies, is this precisely managed, how much more is God managing the spiritual path of your child, whom He created and pursues?

You have to trust that the Father who holds the enormous order of the cosmos also holds the solitary, messy path of your child, even when that path looks dark and illogical to you. He is not overwhelmed by the complexity of the world or the complexity of your family. He is focused on your child's heart, just as the sun is focused on ripening one bunch of grapes.

Ending the Struggle in Surrender

The moment of peace comes when your wrestling ends in surrender. You stop trying to force your timeline onto God, and you choose to trust His superior plan.

The ultimate example of this is Christ in the Garden of Gethsemane. Facing agony, He prayed with deep, honest desire: "Father, take this cup from Me." But He always ended His wrestling with the ultimate surrender: "Not My will, but Yours be done" (Luke 22:42, NASB).

Let your honest wrestling end in that same place. When you feel the pain of the "no" or the "wait," bring it to God, argue your case, shed your tears, and then definitively conclude: "Lord, I don't understand, but Your grace is sufficient. Your will be done in my child's life, and in mine." This is the prayer that stops the agony and starts the enduring work of faith.

References

- Psalm 13:1 (NASB)
- Psalm 10:1 (NASB)
- 2 Corinthians 12:9 (NASB)
- Luke 22:42 (NASB)

Historical and Anecdotal References:

Galileo Galilei Quote: "The sun, with all those planets revolving..." This emphasizes the order and focused attention of the Creator.

- *Source: Attributed to Galileo Galilei.*

Reflection

Take a few minutes to reflect and meditate on what you just read. Write down your thoughts and take time to pray and praise God.

Day 23

Your Role

Defining Your Role: Parent Forever, Protector Never

In the early years of your child's life, your role was clearly defined: you were the shepherd and the protector. You were responsible for setting the walls, managing their choices, and intervening to shield them from consequences.

When your adult child is walking a difficult path, the protective instinct is almost unbearable.

You feel a primal urge to rush in, fix the problem, and save them from the pain. This is where you must execute one of the most painful but necessary spiritual acts: redefining your role.

To find peace and maintain a loving relationship with your adult child, you must firmly accept this new truth: **You are a parent forever**, but you are not a protector forever.

The Shift from Shepherd to Guide

Your relationship must shift from one of control to one of influence. You move from being the Shepherd to being the Guide.

The Old Role: The Shepherd (Control)

As the Shepherd, you had full authority and ultimate responsibility.

You carried the weight of their choices on your own shoulders. When they made a mistake, you had the power to prevent the worst consequences. If you continue to operate as the Shepherd when they are adults, you strip them of the necessary dignity of adulthood, which is freedom of choice and responsibility for consequences.

The New Role: The Guide (Influence)

As the Guide, your job is to influence, love, and model stability. You can offer wisdom, share advice, and point toward the right path (the light on the shore), but they must choose the steps (the journey).

You cannot and should not step between them and the natural, often painful, consequences of their choices.

This is difficult, but consequences are often God's most effective tool for leading a person back to Him.

Consequences are God's way of saying: *"The path you are on does not lead to life."* If you constantly intervene to soften the consequences, you are actually blocking God's primary way of getting their attention.

The book of Proverbs emphasizes the necessity of learning through experience: "The rod and reproof give wisdom, but a child who gets his own way brings shame to his mother" (Proverbs 29:15, NASB).

While your child is now an adult, the spiritual principle holds: true wisdom is forged in the crucible of taking ownership of one's own life.

The Freedom of Boundaries

Defining your role requires the difficult but freeing work of setting healthy boundaries.

A boundary is not a wall to keep your child *out* of your life; it is a fence to keep your own spiritual and emotional health in. It is a statement of what you will and will not do to protect yourself, your marriage, and your relationship with God.

Boundaries allow you to love your child without enabling their destructive behavior. They force your child to confront their own life.

They also give you the emotional space to focus on the work God *has* called you to do—namely, loving your spouse, maintaining your faith, and serving others.

Boundaries should always be focused on **your** actions and stated clearly:

Destructive Attempt at Control	Healthy Boundary (Focus on Self)	Biblical Principle
Endless Arguing: Trying to logically convince them to change their mind.	**Verbal Boundary:** "I will talk about neutral subjects, but I will end the call if you start mocking my faith or arguing with me about my life."	**Be quick to hear, slow to speak** (James 1:19).
Financial Bailing: Constantly paying off debts or providing money for destructive habits.	**Financial Boundary:** "I will not give you cash, but I will pay a utility bill directly, or I will pay for one month of reputable counseling/rehab."	*"For each one will bear his own load"* (Galatians 6:5, NASB).
Emotional Collapse: Allowing your child's mood or crisis to completely destroy your peace.	**Emotional Boundary:** "I love you, but I need two days to process this. I will call you back on Wednesday."	*"Be anxious for nothing"* (Philippians 4:6, NASB).

The Power of Detachment with Love

The goal is detachment with love. This means you detach from the *outcome* of their choices (which is God's business) while remaining attached to them as a person (which is your love).

The Russian novelist Fëdor Dostoevsky (1821–1881), who wrote deeply about human suffering and redemption, spoke of the necessity of self-discovery, observing: "The mystery of human existence lies not just in staying alive, but in finding something to live for."

Your child needs to discover that "something to live for" on their own, often through the pain of hitting rock bottom. If you keep cushioning the fall, you keep them from the place where they are forced to look up and realize they need a different foundation.

Your new role is to hold your ground in love.

Be the stable lighthouse on the shore, not the frantic rescue ship tossed on the waves.

Hold the light of Christ steady, and let them see the way home when they are ready to look. Your enduring, peaceful presence becomes a more powerful guide than any amount of money or emotional manipulation ever could be.

References

- Proverbs 29:15 (NASB)
- Galatians 6:5 (NASB)
- James 1:19 (NASB)
- Philippians 4:6 (NASB)

Historical and Anecdotal References:

- **Fëdor Dostoevsky Quote:** "The mystery of human existence..." This emphasizes the personal responsibility for finding life's purpose beyond mere existence.
    - *Source:* Attributed to Fëdor Dostoevsky.

Reflection

Take a few minutes to reflect and meditate on what you just read. Write down your thoughts and take time to pray and praise God.

Day 24

Marathon

It's a Marathon, Not a Sprint: The Call to Endurance

When the crisis first hits—the dramatic phone call, the unexpected revelation, the final good-bye—you have adrenaline.

You enter a period of sprinting, where you pray constantly, seek counsel frantically, and spend endless energy trying to solve the problem in a weekend.

But when those intense weeks turn into months, and months turn into years, you realize this is not a short, quick battle—it's a spiritual marathon.

The greatest danger in running a marathon is not the pain at the beginning; it's the sheer exhaustion in the middle when you still have a long way to go, and your reserves are depleted. To survive this journey with your faith intact, you must accept the call to endurance—the long, slow, grinding work of faith.

The Necessity of Perseverance

Endurance (or perseverance) is the quality that keeps showing up even when you don't feel like it and when the situation shows no outward signs of improvement. It is the ability to wait patiently on God, knowing that He is working, even when His work is invisible.

The Bible uses the metaphor of a runner to describe the Christian life, and the focus is always on the long haul and the finish line:

"Therefore, since we have so great a cloud of witnesses surrounding us, let us also lay aside every encumbrance and the sin which so easily entangles us, and let us run with endurance the race that is set before us" (Hebrews 12:1, NASB).

You must identify the encumbrance — the heavy baggage of guilt, self-pity, bitterness, or obsession — and consciously lay it aside.

Endurance is about keeping your eyes on the finish line (Christ and His ultimate victory), not on the painful mile marker you are struggling through right now.

God's Timeline vs. Your Timeline

We are people of instant gratification. We want to microwave the miracle.

But God often works through long, slow patience, especially in matters of the heart. Your child's journey back to God might take years of wandering, of hitting the same wall over and over. You have to be okay with God's timeline.

The prophet Habakkuk was so distressed by the timing of God's work that God gave him specific instructions: "Write the vision... and set it clearly on tablets so that one who runs may read it."

And then, the critical instruction for enduring the delay:

"For the vision is yet for the appointed time; it hastens toward the goal and it will not fail. Though it delays, wait for it; for it will certainly come, it will not delay past its appointed time" (Habakkuk 2:2-3, NASB).

The power of this promise is incredible:

God has an appointed time for the resolution, the restoration, and the change in your child's life. It will not delay past that moment. You may not know the date, but you know the Author.

When you feel like you can't wait anymore, remind yourself that you are in a divinely appointed waiting period, and your job is to stay in the race until that time arrives.

Pacing Yourself for the Long Haul

To successfully run a spiritual marathon, you must pace yourself. You can't sprint for a year and then collapse from burnout. Pacing yourself for this long journey means intelligently managing your spiritual, emotional, and physical energy:

1. Practice (Self-Control)

You cannot spend 24 hours a day thinking about your child.

This obsession is a form of spiritual panic that burns you out

Instead, dedicate your energy to things that are productive (prayer, work, marriage) and remove energy from things that are destructive (obsessive news searches, replaying old arguments).

2. Prioritize Spiritual Self-Care (Refueling)

Endurance requires constant refueling. Your spiritual disciplines are the water stops on your race.

If you skip time with God, avoid fellowship, or stop worshiping, you will collapse.

Make a consistent commitment to the Bible, prayer, and Christian community. These activities don't make the pain vanish, but they provide the sustained energy to endure the pain.

3. Rest Without Guilt (Acceptance)

You need physical, mental, and spiritual rest without feeling guilty that you aren't spending every waking moment agonizing over your child.

God commanded the Sabbath rest. Taking a weekend off, going on a date, or simply enjoying a good book is not abandonment; it is stewardship of the only body and mind you have. The most effective endurance runners know when to slow down to make sure they can finish the race.

The famous British Prime Minister Winston Churchill (1874–1965) led his nation through a long, dark war that required immense, sustained courage. He understood the necessity of enduring when the end was nowhere in sight, and the path ahead was terrifying. He is famously credited with the statement:

"If you are going through hell, keep going."

Your life is not hell, but it is certainly a valley of the shadow of death.

Your call is the same: Keep going. Keep praying, keep loving, and keep enduring, because your faithfulness in this long journey is your testimony to a great cloud of witnesses, and it is the very thing that secures your own spiritual victory.

References

- Hebrews 12:1 (NASB)
- Habakkuk 2:2-3 (NASB)
- Romans 8:28 (Implied)
- Revelation 21:4 (Implied)

Historical and Anecdotal References:

Winston Churchill Quote: "If you are going through hell, keep going." This speaks to the necessity of persistence during prolonged difficulty.

- *Source*: Widely attributed to Winston Churchill.

Reflection

Take a few minutes to reflect and meditate on what you just read. Write down your thoughts and take time to pray and praise God.

_____
_____
_____
_____
_____
_____
_____
_____
_____
_____
_____
_____
_____
_____
_____
_____
_____
_____
_____
_____

Day 25

Timing

The Clock on the Wall: God's Timing vs. Our Timing

As parents of a wayward adult child, we often live life looking at two different clocks: Our Timing and God's Timing.

Our Timing is urgent.

It demands an immediate fix to stop the pain, prevent further damage, and guarantee a quick return to safety. Our clock screams: "Fix it now, before it's too late!"

God's Timing is sovereign.

It is calm, precise, and measured according to eternal goals — not just the immediate relief of our feelings. God's clock says: "I will use this exact moment for maximum depth, spiritual maturity, and lasting redemption."

The conflict between these two clocks is the source of nearly all our anxiety. To find peace and endure the long haul, you must learn to deliberately trust the perfect wisdom of God's clock, even when your own is screaming in panic.

The Illusion of Urgency

The belief that you must fix this right now stems from a core mistake: forgetting who holds the power.

When we operate on Our Timing, we act as if God doesn't know the crisis is happening, or that He somehow needs our frantic intervention to succeed.

This urgency often drives the controlling behaviors we discussed earlier: emotional outbursts, ultimatums, or frantic, impulsive attempts to rescue. These actions rarely help the child and always destroy the parent's peace.

The Bible warns against this kind of human haste, comparing it to folly: "The plans of the diligent lead surely to advantage, but everyone who is hasty comes surely to poverty" (Proverbs 21:5, NASB).

When you are spiritually hasty, you come to poverty—you deplete your energy, your faith, and your influence. Waiting on God's Timing, however, is a sign of diligence because it shows you are working according to God's wise plan, not your own emotional demand.

Why God Doesn't Use Our Clock

We often ask, "Why the delay?" God's answer is always rooted in a higher, more complete view of salvation and sanctification. He waits because:

Consequences Must Be Complete:

Redemption often requires that the prodigal fully experience the bitter taste of the consequences of their choices. If God intervened before they reached the end of themselves, they would likely repeat the same mistakes. The prodigal son only came home when he fully realized the shame and emptiness of his situation (Luke 15:17).

Depth Requires Time:

God is not interested in a surface-level behavioral correction; He wants a deep, eternal change of the heart. True spiritual transformation is not an event; it is a long, slow process.

He Is Perfecting Your Faith:

The waiting period is where God strengthens your own spiritual muscles. He uses the wait to teach you dependence, patience, and unwavering trust in His character.

The Absolute Precision of God's Timing

You must come to the conviction that God's timing is not just "better" than yours; it is perfect. It is never early, and it is never late. Every moment of this waiting period is being used for a purpose in both your child's life and your own.

The Old Testament prophet Isaiah gave a powerful promise about the nature of God's intervention: "Therefore the Lord longs to be gracious to you, and therefore He waits on high to have compassion on you. For the Lord is a God of justice; how blessed are all those who wait for Him" (Isaiah 30:18, NASB).

This verse is a profound insight into God's heart:

He waits on high:

God is not passive; He is actively watching and ready to act.

He longs to be gracious:

God wants to step in and show compassion. He is not stalling out of indifference.

He is a God of justice:

His timing is perfect because it aligns with His righteous plan. It will happen at the most just and redemptive moment.

Therefore, when you feel anxious about the delay, remind yourself: God is waiting because the perfect moment for maximum grace and justice has not yet arrived. The moment you see as a delay, God sees as the last, necessary step before intervention.

The Parable of the Seed and the Soil

Think of God's timing like a farmer planting a seed. The farmer cannot rush the harvest. He must wait patiently while the seed (your prayer, your influence, the child's consequences) undergoes an invisible, slow transformation in the dark soil (their heart).

If the farmer panicked and dug up the seed every day to check on it, he would ruin the process.

The Apostle James uses this exact analogy to encourage Christians enduring hardship: "Be patient, therefore, brethren, until the coming of the Lord. The farmer waits for the precious produce of the soil, being patient about it, until it gets the early and late rains" (James 5:7, NASB).

Your job is to be the patient farmer. You have planted the seed of faith and prayer. You must now patiently wait for the spiritual rain (the Holy Spirit's work) and the appointed time of harvest, trusting the Creator who understands the soil better than you do.

The Practice of Waiting

Waiting is an act of faith, and faith requires action. You do not wait passively; you wait actively.

<u>1. Exchange Anxiety for Expectation</u>

Instead of using the waiting time for worry, use it for expectant hope. Worry drains; expectation fuels. Every time the thought "Will this ever change?" enters your mind, immediately replace it with the statement: "I know I will reap if I do not grow weary, for God's time will certainly come" (Galatians 6:9, NASB, adapted).

<u>2. Live in Today's Grace</u>

The philosopher Søren Kierkegaard (1813-1855) wrote deeply about the anxiety of human existence. He taught that peace is found in focusing on the present moment. Worry is often trying to manage tomorrow's problems with only today's grace.

God only promises grace for today. "The steadfast love of the Lord never ceases; His mercies never come to an end; they are new every morning; great is Your faithfulness" (Lamentations 3:22-23, NASB).

Surrender your anxiety over next month's crisis and focus on receiving the fresh, new mercy God is offering you for the next six hours. This focus prevents burnout and honors God's faithful provision.

<u>3. Seek the Glimpses of His Work</u>

God does not leave you without clues. During the waiting, look actively for the glimpses of His work—a small, positive step your child takes, a kind word spoken, a moment of sobriety, or simply the continued conviction of your own heart to pray.

These small signs are reminders that the seed is still active beneath the soil, and God's clock is steadily ticking toward His perfect appointment.

Choose to align your heart with God's perfect timing. Rest in the knowledge that the delay you fear is actually the careful, loving patience of a Father working to save your child and refine your faith.

References

- Proverbs 21:5 (NASB)
- Luke 15:17 (Implied)
- Isaiah 30:18 (NASB)
- James 5:7 (NASB)
- Galatians 6:9 (NASB, adapted)
- Lamentations 3:22–23 (NASB)

Historical and Anecdotal References:

Søren Kierkegaard: His focus on anxiety and the present moment is a powerful antidote to future-based worry.

  o *Source:* Based on themes in Kierkegaard's work, particularly his focus on the self and existence.

Reflection

Take a few minutes to reflect and meditate on what you just read. Write down your thoughts and take time to pray and praise God.

_____
_____
_____
_____
_____
_____
_____
_____
_____
_____
_____
_____
_____
_____
_____
_____

Day 26

Why Pray

Why Pray? The Assurance of God's Hearing

When you are praying for your wayward adult child, the most frequent question that sneaks into your mind is often the simplest: Why bother?

You may feel like your prayers are hitting the ceiling, or that your words are too weak to change the massive, destructive course your child is on. You might ask: If God is sovereign and already knows the end, why do I need to ask Him for it?

This chapter is about establishing the non-negotiable truth: Prayer is not optional; it is the single most powerful tool God has given you. It is the direct line to the only One who can truly change the situation. The reason **you pray is not to inform God, but to engage God** in your struggle and align your weak human will with His powerful divine will.

1. The Divine Invitation: God Wants to Hear You

The primary reason you pray is not a duty, but a privilege—it is God's invitation for you to speak to Him. He is not a distant, annoyed ruler; He is a loving Father who literally commands us to talk to Him.

The Apostle Paul tells us to bring our most specific, crushing anxieties to Him:

"Be anxious for nothing, but in everything by prayer and supplication with thanksgiving let your requests be made known to God. And the peace of God, which surpasses all comprehension, will guard your hearts and your minds in Christ Jesus" (Philippians 4:6-7, NASB).

Notice the exchange: You trade anxiety for requests. You do not overcome worry by sheer willpower; you overcome it by diverting it into prayer. When you pray for your child, you are not just hoping for a change in their life; you are receiving a guaranteed peace in your own life.

Prayer is the channel through which God pours His peace into your anxious heart.

2. Prayer Changes the One Who Prays

We often think of prayer as a one-way street meant only to change the person we are praying for (our child). But the first and most immediate person prayer changes is you.

In the long, difficult journey of enduring a prodigal child, prayer does these vital things for your soul:

It builds Dependence: When you pray, you confess that you are powerless, and God is all-powerful. This humility is the bedrock of Christian maturity.

It Fights Bitterness: It is impossible to hold deep resentment against your child while simultaneously praying for their salvation and well-being. Prayer forces you to choose love over bitterness.

It Aligns Your Heart: As you pray for God's will to be done, your focus shifts from your short-sighted, impatient desires to God's wise, redemptive purpose.

The great Christian author C.S. Lewis once remarked on the power of prayer in shaping the petitioner: "I pray because I can't help myself. I pray because I'm helpless. I pray because the need flows out of me all the time — waking and sleeping. It doesn't change God. It changes me."

You pray because you are helpless, and that very act of helplessness is what unlocks God's peace in your life.

3. Prayer is the Engine of Change

While prayer changes you, the Bible is also clear that prayer is the catalyst God uses to enact His will on earth. God, in His sovereignty, has chosen to limit Himself to working through the petitions of His people.

The book of James gives us an astonishing promise about the physical power of prayer:

"The effective prayer of a righteous man can accomplish much" (James 5:16, NASB).

The word translated as "effective" implies an energy, a power, a sustained, fervent effort. Your prayer for your child is not a casual wish; it is a spiritual force that accomplishes much in the invisible realm.

When you pray, you are praying for God to send people into your child's life.

You are praying for the Holy Spirit to convict their heart.

You are praying for obstacles to be placed in the way of destructive choices.

You are praying for the circumstances to align in a way that leads them back to repentance.

Prayer is your highest, most effective form of action. It is the work God called you to do when you had run out of all other human options. Never underestimate the power of a parent's persistent, loving prayer. It is the spiritual engine of change for your child's life.

References

- Philippians 4:6–7 (NASB)
- James 5:16 (NASB)

Historical and Anecdotal References:

C.S. Lewis Quote: "I pray because I can't help myself..." This quote emphasizes the effect of prayer on the petitioner's own heart and dependence on God.

- *Source:* Attributed to C.S. Lewis.

Reflection

Take a few minutes to reflect and meditate on what you just read. Write down your thoughts and take time to pray and praise God.

Day 27

When to Pray

When Should I Pray? The Rhythm of Persistence

If prayer is the engine of change, the next logical question is: When should I pray for my child? Should it be a burst of intense prayer followed by long periods of silence, or a continuous, low-level flow?

The answer is that you need a rhythm of persistence—scheduled, committed moments of focused prayer combined with a spontaneous, constant state of reliance on God throughout your day.

<u>1. The Call to Persistent, Scheduled Prayer</u>

In the crisis of a wayward child, prayer cannot be relegated to a last resort or an occasional thought. It must be a disciplined, committed appointment on your calendar. This discipline is taught clearly by Jesus Himself.

Jesus told a parable about a persistent widow who kept coming to a powerful, unjust judge until he finally granted her request, simply because she was persistent. Jesus concluded the parable with this instruction:

"Now will not God bring about justice for His elect who cry to Him day and night, and will He delay long over them? I tell you that He will bring about justice for them quickly" (Luke 18:7-8, NASB).

The lesson here is not that God is an unjust judge, but that if persistence works on a bad judge, how much more will it work on a good Father? The call is to "cry to Him day and night."

The Practical Application: Commit to a specific time every day to pray for your child—10 minutes in the morning, 5 minutes before bed. This scheduled time ensures that no matter how busy or tired you are, you are persistently engaging the power of God. This routine makes prayer a cornerstone of your endurance, not just a frantic reaction.

2. Pray in Every Moment: The State of Constant Reliance

While scheduled prayer is essential, the Bible also encourages a constant, fluid communication with God that permeates your entire day. This is often called "praying without ceasing."

The Apostle Paul gave this command to the believers in Thessalonica: "Rejoice always; pray without ceasing; in everything give thanks; for this is God's will for you in Christ Jesus" (1 Thessalonians 5:16–18, NASB).

How do you pray without ceasing? This doesn't mean you are saying full, formal prayers every minute. It means living in a constant state of reliance on God, where every thought, worry, and moment of gratitude is instantly redirected to Him.

When the phone rings and you see your child's name, that is the moment to pray a one-second prayer: "Lord, guide my words and protect my heart."

When a wave of fear washes over you, that is the moment to pray: "Father, I cast this anxiety on You now."

When you see something beautiful, that is the moment to pray: "Thank You, God, for this glimpse of Your goodness."

This constant prayer turns your whole day into an act of worship and spiritual vigilance. It is the spiritual air you breathe, ensuring you never carry the burden alone for long.

3. Pray When You Don't Want To

The time when you feel least like praying is often the time when you most need to pray. When weariness, apathy, or bitterness sets in, the devil wants you to stop praying.

The spiritual battle is often won simply by showing up. When you feel too tired, too defeated, or too angry to pray, your prayer can be the simplest possible plea: "Jesus, help me. I have nothing left, but I am showing up anyway."

The great 17th-century devotional writer Brother Lawrence emphasized that constant communication with God should be woven into every task, no matter how small or mundane. He taught that the simplest tasks—like washing dishes—become an act of worship when done with conscious reference to God.

If you can find God in the quiet act of service, you can certainly find Him in the urgent need to pray for your child. Make prayer an unbreakable habit that endures all seasons of emotional fatigue.

References

- Luke 18:7-8 (NASB)
- 1 Thessalonians 5:16-18 (NASB)

Historical and Anecdotal References:

Brother Lawrence: His practice of the presence of God emphasizes weaving prayer into daily life.

- *Source:* The Practice of the Presence of God.

Reflection

Take a few minutes to reflect and meditate on what you just read. Write down your thoughts and take time to pray and praise God.

Day 28

How to Pray

How Should I Pray? Aligning Your Words with His Will

Once you are convinced of *why* and *when* to pray, the most practical struggle remains: How should I pray?

You may find yourself running out of words, or simply repeating the same desperate pleas, unsure if you are even praying correctly.

To pray effectively, you must learn to shift your prayers from human demands (focused on outcomes *you* want) to divine alignment (focused on the redemptive will *God* has revealed).

<u>1. Praying Scripture: Using God's Own Words</u>

When you run out of words, the single best source for prayer is the Bible itself. When you pray scripture, you are confident that you are praying exactly in line with God's will, because you are using His own inspired language.
There are three key areas of scripture to use when praying for your wayward child:

A. Praying for Salvation and Conviction

It is always God's will that none should perish. Pray His own words for your child's heart:
- *"Father, Your Word says You are patient toward all, not wishing for any to perish, but for all to come to repentance (2 Peter 3:9, NASB). I claim that promise over my child's heart today."*
- *"Lord, I pray that You will grant my child repentance leading to the knowledge of the truth, and that they will come to their senses and escape the snare of the devil (2 Timothy 2:25–26, NASB)."*

B. Praying for Your Peace and Strength

The crisis is straining your soul. Pray for your own endurance:
- *"God, help me to walk by the Spirit so I will not carry out the desires of the flesh (Galatians 5:16, NASB) – the flesh that tempts me to worry, rage, or despair."*
- *"Lord, fill me with all joy and peace in believing, so that I will abound in hope by the power of the Holy Spirit (Romans 15:13, NASB)."*

C. Praying for God's Provision

Pray for God to actively intervene in their circumstances:
- *"Lord, I pray that Your hand would be upon my child for good (Ezra 7:9, NASB), and that You would direct their steps (Proverbs 3:5-6, NASB, adapted) even when they are walking away."*

2. Praying the "How" and "What" of the Crisis

You can structure your prayers by deliberately working through the different aspects of the crisis:

Focus Area	How to Pray	Why it is Effective
Their Mind	Pray for their minds to be cleared of lies and destructive thoughts. Pray that the "god of this world has blinded" (2 Corinthians 4:4, NASB) them, and that You would remove the spiritual blindness.	Addresses the root of destructive behavior: spiritual deception.
Their Relationships	Pray that God will remove destructive influences (bad friends, toxic partners) and send godly people (mentors, new friends) into their path at the right moment.	Invites God's active, circumstantial intervention in their social network.
Their Rock Bottom	Pray for clear consequences (not rescue). Pray that they reach the end of their own resources so that they are forced to look up and realize their need for God (Luke 15:17).	This is a risky, hard prayer, but it trusts God's perfect, disciplinary love more than your own fear.

3. The Power of "Not My Will, But Yours"

Ultimately, the most powerful words you can pray are those of surrender. This means moving your prayers away from *"Please change this immediately"* to *"Please use this perfectly."*

The core of prayer is aligning our will with the perfect will of God. The Jesuit founder Saint Ignatius of Loyola (1491–1556) developed a model of prayer that emphasized complete surrender to God's plan, regardless of the cost. He taught that we must pray with total trust in the Father's greater wisdom.

"Take, Lord, and receive all my liberty, my memory, my understanding, and my entire will, all I have and call my own. You have given all to me. To you, Lord, I return it. Everything is yours; do with it what you will. Give me only your love and your grace, that is enough for me." Saint Ignatius of Loyola

Jesus showed us this model in the Garden of Gethsemane:
"Father, if You are willing, remove this cup from Me; yet not My will, but Yours be done" (Luke 22:42, NASB).

When you pray for your child, end your plea with that simple, brave submission. This is the prayer that stops the agony of trying to control the situation and gives you the peace of knowing the outcome is now in the hands of a loving, sovereign God.

References
- 2 Peter 3:9 (NASB)
- 2 Timothy 2:25-26 (NASB)
- Galatians 5:16 (NASB)
- Romans 15:13 (NASB)
- Ezra 7:9 (NASB)
- Proverbs 3:5-6 (NASB, adapted)
- 2 Corinthians 4:4 (NASB)
- Luke 15:17 (Implied)
- Luke 22:42 (NASB)

Historical and Anecdotal References:

- Saint Ignatius of Loyola: Known for emphasizing complete surrender to God's will in prayer.
    - *Source:* Based on the teachings of Ignatius of Loyola.

Reflection

Take a few minutes to reflect and meditate on what you just read. Write down your thoughts and take time to pray and praise God.

Day 29

Where to Pray

Where Should I Pray? The Power of Proximity

The final question about prayer is a practical one: Where should I pray? While God hears your prayers no matter where you are, your physical location and emotional posture dramatically affect your ability to pray with focus, faith, and persistence.

This chapter explores the power of proximity—how intentionally choosing where you pray can deepen your connection to God and to your community.

1. The Personal Sanctuary: The Power of Solitude

Jesus modeled the power of finding a private place—a sanctuary—to pray away from the distractions and demands of the world. He often withdrew to a solitary place to talk with His Father.

The goal of your personal sanctuary is to create a place of quiet devotion where you can be totally honest with God about your pain, fear, and love.

"But you, when you pray, go into your inner room, close your door and pray to your Father who is in secret, and your Father who sees what is done in secret will reward you" (Matthew 6:6, NASB).

Your "inner room" could be a corner of your home, a favorite chair, or even your car.

The place itself isn't magical, but the discipline of retreating is. When you close the door on your distractions (phone, work, household chores), you open the door to focused, persistent prayer. This is the place where you practice vulnerability and wrestle with God honestly.

2. The Shared Sanctuary: The Power of Corporate Prayer

While solitary prayer is essential, you were not meant to carry this burden alone. You gain powerful spiritual strength when you gather with other believers to pray, especially with those who understand your specific pain (as discussed in the fellowship chapter).

Jesus gave a special promise to those who gather in His name:

"Again I say to you, that if two of you agree on earth about anything that they may ask, it shall be done for them by My Father who is in heaven. For where two or three have gathered in My name, I am there in their midst" (Matthew 18:19-20, NASB).

The power of corporate prayer is not just in the numbers, but in the agreement. When you pray with another Christian parent for your child, you are leveraging shared faith and inviting Christ's promised presence.

Pray with your spouse: This is the most crucial corporate prayer. It unifies your marriage and ensures you are fighting the same battle on the same spiritual front.

Pray in a support group: Praying in a group specifically for parents of prodigals gives you the confidence that your agreement is based on genuine empathy and shared burden.

3. The Battlefield: Praying In Situ

Sometimes, the most powerful place to pray is right in the middle of the crisis itself — the Battlefield. This means praying in situ, or "on the spot."

- When you are about to have a difficult conversation with your child, pray in your heart right before you speak.

- When you are standing in your child's empty bedroom, pray over the space.

- When you drive past a place that represents a past mistake or current danger, pray over that location.

The great missionary Amy Carmichael (1867–1951), who worked in dangerous and often heartbreaking circumstances, stressed the need for constant, practical prayer in the face of need. She understood that our spiritual weapons must be deployed right where the battle is fiercest.

Praying in situ turns a moment of crisis into a moment of spiritual engagement. It replaces panic with power and fear with faith.

The Posture of Prayer

Finally, remember that the posture of your heart is always more important than the posture of your body. God hears you whether you are standing, sitting, kneeling, or driving.

However, intentionally changing your physical posture can affect your emotional state:

Kneeling: Represents humility and complete surrender to God's sovereignty.

Standing: Represents readiness and spiritual vigilance.

Open Hands: Represents receiving God's grace and releasing your grip on the problem.

Choose a time, a place, and a posture that best allows you to meet the God of all comfort and engage the Father of mercies on behalf of your beloved child.

References

- Matthew 6:6 (NASB)
- Matthew 18:19–20 (NASB)

Historical and Anecdotal References:

Amy Carmichael: Her life models prayer and action in difficult situations.

- *Source*: Based on the life and work of Amy Carmichael.

Reflection

Take a few minutes to reflect and meditate on what you just read. Write down your thoughts and take time to pray and praise God.

Day 30

Forgiveness

The Parent's Release: Forgiveness as Freedom

You have endured the pain, established boundaries, and surrendered control to God. Yet, there remains a spiritual weight that can anchor you to bitterness: unforgiveness.

When your adult child has wounded you deeply — through disrespect, betrayal, addiction, or simply walking away from all you hold dear — the natural human reaction is to hold onto resentment. You feel entitled to that anger; after all, you were the victim.

But here is the absolute truth: Forgiveness is not a feeling, and it is not a transaction. It is a conscious, spiritual decision you make in your heart and mind, releasing the debt, not for their sake, but for your own freedom.

Even though your prodigal child has not asked for it, and may never ask for it, you must choose to forgive to complete your own journey of healing.

The Prisoner of Resentment

Just like bitterness, holding onto unforgiveness is like drinking poison and expecting the other person to die. The resentment does not hurt your child; it only binds **you** to the pain and the choices they made. It gives them, and the devil, continued control over your emotional life.

The great Christian missionary and teacher Corrie ten Boom (1892-1983) survived the horrors of a Nazi concentration camp. She witnessed suffering and evil on a scale few of us can imagine, yet she spoke with profound authority about forgiveness: "If you have forgiven all who injured you, you live in peace."

Corrie ten Boom understood that peace is the reward of forgiveness. If you want to live in peace, you must free your heart from the prison of resentment.

What Forgiveness Is and Is Not

To execute this internal release, you must clearly define what Christian forgiveness is:

Forgiveness IS NOT...	Forgiveness IS...
Forgetting: You will likely always remember the pain; forgiveness means the **memory loses its power to control you.**	**A Decision:** It is a choice of the will to cancel the debt your child owes you for the hurt they caused.
A Feeling: You may never *feel* warm and fuzzy about the offense; forgiveness is a **spiritual act of obedience** regardless of emotion.	**Releasing the Debt:** You hand the right to vengeance and justice over to God, where it belongs.
Reconciliation: It does not mean you must immediately restore the relationship to its old form or remove boundaries. Forgiveness is **internal**; reconciliation requires repentance from the other person.	**A Process:** It is often a daily, sometimes hourly, choice to release the resentment as the memory surfaces.

The Biblical Command: Forgiving as We Are Forgiven

The core motivation for forgiving your child is not because they deserve it, but because you were forgiven an infinitely greater debt.

Jesus made this clear in the Lord's Prayer: "And forgive us our debts, as we also have forgiven our debtors" (Matthew 6:12, NASB).

The Apostle Paul amplified this command, linking our personal peace directly to the forgiveness we have received from God:

"Be kind to one another, tender-hearted, forgiving each other, just as God in Christ also has forgiven you" (Ephesians 4:32, NASB).

When you choose to hold onto bitterness toward your child, you are essentially telling God, *"The forgiveness You gave me was not sufficient to cover the pain this child caused me."* This dishonors the vast, free gift of salvation and forgiveness you received in Christ.

Forgiving your child is the ultimate act of humility—admitting that your anger, while justified, is a small thing compared to the cosmic debt Christ paid for you.

Handing Over the Scales of Justice

The greatest difficulty in forgiving a prodigal is the feeling that you are letting them "get away with it." This is where you must actively practice surrender (as discussed in the previous chapter).

You are not the judge. You are commanded to turn over the scales of justice to God. The Bible explicitly warns us against trying to exact our own revenge:

"Never take your own revenge, beloved, but leave room for the wrath *of God*, for it is written, 'VENGEANCE IS MINE, I WILL REPAY,' says the Lord" (Romans 12:19, NASB).

When you forgive your child, you are simply saying: *"God, I release my right to hold this wrong against them. I trust that Your justice and Your mercy are perfect, and I leave their accountability in Your hands."* This is an act of total trust in God's sovereignty.

Practical Steps to Execute Forgiveness

Since forgiveness is a decision of the will, you can practice it through deliberate, repeatable steps:

<u>1. Identify the Specific Debt</u>

Don't just forgive the vague concept of "hurt." Name the specific actions that caused the wound: *I forgive them for the betrayal of my trust. I forgive them for the shame they caused my family. I forgive them for the financial burden they left me with.* Naming the debt makes the release concrete.

2. Pray the Release

Go to your private place of prayer (your sanctuary) and speak the words of release out loud. Use simple, definitive language: "Lord, I choose to forgive [Child's Name] for [Specific Action]. I release the right to hold this against them, and I trust You to handle their ultimate accountability. I do this so that I may be free."

3. Repeat as Necessary

The initial decision to forgive is crucial, but the feeling of resentment will often return. Every time the memory or the accompanying wave of pain arises, repeat the forgiveness prayer.

Do not dwell on the memory. Immediately interrupt the thought with the spoken declaration: "I already forgave that debt. I choose to release it again in Jesus' name." This trains your mind to accept the completed transaction of forgiveness.

4. Forgive Yourself

Often, the hardest person to forgive is yourself — for the mistakes you made, the things you didn't see, or the ways you weren't perfect.

This self-condemnation is just as destructive as resentment toward your child. Remember: "There is now no condemnation for those who are in Christ Jesus" (Romans 8:1, NASB). If God has forgiven you, you have the spiritual authority to forgive yourself.

Choose your peace over your pain. Choose freedom over bondage. Choose to forgive your child, even though they haven't asked, and step forward unburdened by resentment.

References

- Matthew 6:12 (NASB)
- Ephesians 4:32 (NASB)
- Romans 12:19 (NASB)
- Romans 8:1 (NASB)

Historical and Anecdotal References:

- **Corrie ten Boom Quote:** "If you have forgiven all who injured you, you live in peace." This quote reflects her message after surviving the Holocaust.

    o *Source:* Corrie ten Boom, *The Hiding Place* (Implied context).

Reflection

Take a few minutes to reflect and meditate on what you just read. Write down your thoughts and take time to pray and praise God.

_____
_____
_____
_____
_____
_____
_____
_____
_____
_____
_____
_____
_____
_____
_____
_____
_____
_____
_____
_____

Day 31

Your Identity

Unchanging Value: Where Your Identity Truly Rests

Throughout this journey with a wayward adult child, you have battled fear, exhaustion, and shame. All these corrosive emotions attack one central thing: **your identity.**

The world, and even your own tired mind, whispers a painful lie: *"If your child is failing, then you are a failure."* You may feel defined by your child's choices, your family's brokenness, or your inability to "fix" the situation. This chapter is a call to stand on the single most comforting and non-negotiable truth in the universe:

Your identity is not found in your performance as a parent; it is found entirely in your position as a child of God. What God says about you is the only definition that matters, regardless of what your circumstances — or your child — might say.

The Cracked Mirror of Circumstance

If you try to determine who you are based on your circumstances, you are looking into a cracked mirror that gives you a distorted, painful image.

- Circumstance says: "You raised a child who left the faith. You are a bad parent."
- The World says: "Your life is messy. You are a source of gossip or pity."
- Shame says: "You failed to protect them. You are guilty."

When you try to find your worth in the *reflection* of your family life, your value will constantly rise and fall with every decision your child makes. This is an unsustainable, exhausting way to live.

The Problem of Defining Yourself by Outcome

For many Christian parents, identity becomes dangerously tied to the outcome of their parenting—the successful, well-adjusted, faithful adult child.

When that outcome doesn't materialize, the foundation of your self-worth crumbles. But God never intended for your worth to be based on an outcome you cannot control. The Bible defines your identity entirely by the action of God in your life.

The Apostle Paul is clear: you are not identified by your performance, but by God's choice to adopt you.

"He predestined us to adoption as sons through Jesus Christ to Himself, according to the kind intention of His will" (Ephesians 1:5, NASB).

You are a child of God not because of your goodness, discipline, or perfect parenting, but according to the kind intention of His will. Your adoption certificate is signed by God and cannot be revoked by the actions of your earthly child.

The Unchanging Truths of Your Identity

When you feel doubt creeping in, you must deliberately replace the lie with the unshakable, unchanging truth of who God says you are.

Lie (Circumstance)	Truth (God's Word)
You are a failure.	You are forgiven.
You are weak.	You are God's chosen one.
You are defined by this crisis.	You are defined by Christ.

Here are three foundational truths about your identity that cannot be altered by your child's choices:

1. You Are Chosen and Holy

You are not an accident, and your situation is not a mistake. You were chosen by God for this specific time and place.

"So, as those who have been chosen of God, holy and beloved, put on a heart of compassion, kindness, humility, gentleness and patience" (Colossians 3:12, NASB).

Notice the order: God calls you chosen, holy, and beloved *before* He tells you to put on compassion and patience. Your value is established before your actions are commanded. You don't have to earn your holiness by perfectly navigating this crisis; you live *from* that holiness.

2. You Are a New Creation

You are not the same parent who made mistakes twenty years ago. The old guilt and the past failures do not define you.

"Therefore if anyone is in Christ, he is a new creature; the old things passed away; behold, new things have come" (2 Corinthians 5:17, NASB).

When the past failures flood your mind—the harsh words, the impatience, the things you wish you had done differently—you must declare this truth: The old things have passed away. You are a new creation. You are forgiven, and you are starting today with fresh grace.

3. You Are Perfectly Loved

Your child's love may feel conditional, absent, or painful. God's love is none of those things. It is perfect, persistent, and unshakeable.

The great theologian Martin Luther (1483-1546), when battling doubt, would affirm his identity by writing the words *'Baptizatus Sum'* (I am Baptized). This reminded him that he was eternally marked as God's own.

You must do the same. If you know Christ, you are beloved. There is nothing your child can do—good or bad—that will make God love you more or less.

"Who will separate us from the love of Christ? Will tribulation, or distress, or persecution, or famine, or nakedness, or peril, or sword?" (Romans 8:35, NASB).

The answer is a triumphant "No!" No crisis, no distance, and no pain has the power to separate you from the love of God. Your spiritual well-being is secure, even when your earthly reality is chaotic.

The Freedom of Identity

Accepting this truth—that your worth is in Christ alone—is incredibly freeing.

<u>It frees you from the Need to Control.</u> If your identity is not tied to your child's success, you no longer need to manipulate or fix their life to prove your worth. You are free to simply love them and influence them without the crushing pressure of needing to save them.

<u>It frees you from the Fear of Judgment.</u> When people judge you, you can kindly acknowledge their opinion, knowing that their assessment has no authority over your identity. You are defined by the God who sees your heart, not the neighbor who sees your situation.

The famous French philosopher and scientist Blaise Pascal (1623–1662) captured the human longing for fulfillment, noting that there is a "God-shaped vacuum" in the heart of every person that only God can fill. You cannot fill that vacuum with your child's success, a perfect family, or the world's approval.

The peace you seek in this journey is found when you stop trying to earn your worth and instead rest completely in the eternal, unchanging truth of who God says you already are: Chosen, holy, new, and beloved. This is your secure identity. Live from it.

References

- Ephesians 1:5 (NASB)
- Colossians 3:12 (NASB)
- 2 Corinthians 5:17 (NASB)
- Romans 8:35 (NASB)

Historical and Anecdotal References:

- **Martin Luther Quote:** The concept of 'Baptizatus Sum' (I am Baptized) as an affirmation of identity in Christ.
    - *Source:* Based on Luther's life and theological practice.

- **Blaise Pascal Quote:** The concept of the "God-shaped vacuum" in human existence.
    - *Source:* Attributed to Blaise Pascal, *Pensées*.

Paul Beersdorf

Reflection

Take a few minutes to reflect and meditate on what you just read. Write down your thoughts and take time to pray and praise God.

Epilogue:
Your Love, God's Story

You have reached the end of these pages, but you are still walking the path of faith and grief. You've wrestled with the hard truths about control, surrendered your anxiety, and committed to showing up in community.

As you close this book and step back into the reality of your daily life, remember the single most important truth that covers everything we have discussed:

Your love for your child is real, but your love is not the anchor. God's faithfulness is.

The temptation to despair will come again.

The difficult phone calls will happen. The fear that you did not do enough will whisper in the dark. In those moments, do not look inward at your capacity, or backward at your mistakes.

Look upward to the one who is able to do immeasurably more than all we ask or imagine.

A Final Charge for the Journey

Here is your final, simple charge—a way to integrate everything you have learned into a sustainable rhythm of faith:

Stop Trying to Control the Ocean, Start Steering Your Ship (Self-Control & Influence): Accept that your child's choices are the ocean (God's territory). Your energy must be used to steer your own ship—your marriage, your peace, your words, and your reactions. Focus on influence (prayer, peace, example), not control (force, manipulation, argument).

Trade Isolation for Intention (Fellowship & Vulnerability):

The enemy wins when you hide. Choose to be seen by your spouse, your friends, and your church. Your vulnerability is not a weakness; it is the doorway through which God sends His comfort.

Frame Your Present in Eternity (Promises & Hope):

Your current pain is real, but it is temporary. Live every day framed by the promise that God works all things together for good (Romans 8:28, NASB) and that a day is coming when all tears will be wiped away (Revelation 21:4, NASB). This ultimate hope makes today's endurance possible.

Parent, your journey is a unique and challenging demonstration of enduring love. The greatest testimony you will ever give is not the story of your perfect family, but the story of how you held onto Jesus when your family looked broken.

Your child is not a closed case. Their story is still being written, and God is the author.

Surrender the pen to Him, and rest in His peace.

Final Verse of Assurance
"Now may the God of hope fill you with all joy and peace in believing, so that you will abound in hope by the power of the Holy Spirit." (Romans 15:13, NASB)

Go in peace. You are seen. You are loved. And you are not alone.

Summary

Summary: Lessons for the Journey

You have walked through 31 days of intense focus, wrestling with the most painful questions a parent can face. This chapter is a summary—a quick reference guide—to remind you of the essential truths and key actions that will sustain your hope as you continue this spiritual marathon.

Part I: The Foundational Truths
(Days 1, 18, 22, 25, 30,31)

Before you can act, you must believe. These chapters remind you where your true value lies and how to think correctly about your situation.

Part II: The Inner Work and Discipline
(Days 2, 4, 7, 9, 13, 16, 17, 23)

These chapters focus on the actions you can take to maintain your inner stability when external circumstances are chaotic.

Part III: The Community and Endurance
 (Days 3, 5, 8, 14, 15, 10, 11, 12, 24)

These chapters, charge you to keep living, keep connecting, and draw strength from your community.

Part IV: The Prayer Life
(Days 26, 27, 28, 29, 6, 19, 20, 21)

These chapters summarize the foundation and framework for your most vital spiritual practice.

Day 1: The Loss You must acknowledge and name your grief. You are mourning the loss of the present relationship AND the **death of the future dream** you carried for your family.

Key Point: There is a time to mourn (Ecclesiastes 3:4). Don't hide the **shame** or pain.

Key Action: Allow the wave of grief to push you against the **Rock of Ages** (Christ) for support.

Day 2: Be Still You must deliberately unplug from the fear and noise of your grief. This mental stillness is required to hear the reassuring, quiet voice of God.

Key Point: The command is to **stop striving** and know that God is God (Psalm 46:10).

Key Action: Create a **sacred silence spot** to consciously quiet your mind and focus on God's presence.

Day 3: Don't Give Up Your spiritual strength is measured by the **steadiness of your hope**. You must keep praying and believing even when all evidence points toward failure.

Key Point: The Lord will bring about justice for those who **cry to Him day and night** (Luke 18:7–8).

Key Action: Refuse to let your current reality redefine God's character or diminish your **hope**.

Day 4: Don't Give In You are called to hold both grace and truth. Do not compromise your core biblical values to maintain an illusion of peace or affirm destructive choices.

Key Point: Grace without truth is meaningless. You are full of **grace and truth** (John 1:14).

Key Action: Set **biblical boundaries** on your home and resources, but never stop loving the person.

Day 5: Life Goes On Continuing to live your life fully — working, engaging your other family, and serving — is an act of **courageous obedience** and trust in God.

Key Point: **"Prepare your minds for action"** (1 Peter 1:13, NASB). Your life has meaning beyond this crisis.

Key Action: Cherish and protect the family and relationships you **still have** today.

Day 6: Be at Peace Peace is the **anchor** that holds your ship steady in the storm, not just something you find when the storm is over. It is the result of engaging spiritual disciplines.

Key Point: God's peace guards your **hearts and minds** in Christ Jesus (Philippians 4:7).

Key Action: Practice **active expectation**, resting in the certain knowledge of God's sovereignty.

Day 7: Take Every Thought Captive The battle for your peace is fought in your mind. Every fearful or condemning thought must be **captured** and **replaced** with God's truth.

Key Point: **"Take every thought captive to the obedience of Christ"** (2 Corinthians 10:5, NASB).

Key Action: Practice the **4-Step Plan**: Intercept the lie, check it against Scripture, replace it with the truth, and stand firm.

Day 8: Seek Wise Counsel You cannot walk this painful path alone. Seeking counsel is a sign of **humble strength** that allows light and wisdom into your situation.

Key Point: **"Without consultation, plans go awry, but with many counselors they succeed"** (Proverbs 15:22, NASB).

Key Action: Find a trusted Christian counselor, elder, or mentor whose advice is **rooted in Scripture**.

Day 8: Beware of Bitterness & Envy Bitterness poisons your soul and ties you to the wound. Envy challenges God's goodness by focusing on the success of others. Both are sins that block healing.

Key Point: Bitterness is a **root** that must be pulled up to avoid contaminating others (Hebrews 12:15).

Key Action: Immediately turn every thought of envy into a **prayer of sincere blessing** for the person you are envying.

Day 10: Fellowship Your community is your spiritual lifeline. The church provides the **spiritual fire** that keeps your faith burning when you are exhausted and cold.

Key Point: Do not neglect meeting together, but **encourage one another** (Hebrews 10:24–25).

Key Action: Commit to attending church, even when you don't feel like it, to receive necessary **encouragement**.

Day 11: Friends Trusted friends offer perspective, vital support, and necessary **distraction** from the overwhelming weight of the crisis.

Key Point: A friend loves at all times, and a brother is **born for adversity** (Proverbs 17:17).

Key Action: Identify one or two **safe friends** and be honest with them about your pain.

Day 12: Family You must fiercely **protect your marriage** as your primary vow and cherish the other children and family members who depend on your stability.

Key Point: Two are better than one, and a **threefold cord is not quickly broken** (Ecclesiastes 4:9–12).

Key Action: Schedule regular, intentional time with your spouse and healthy children, prioritizing their emotional needs.

Day 13: Self-Control When everything external is out of control, you must focus on the one thing God has given you the power to manage: **your own reactions** and emotions.

Key Point: God gave you the Spirit of power, love, and **discipline** (self-control) (2 Timothy 1:7).

Key Action: Practice the **pause** before reacting to difficult texts or conversations, and refuse to be governed by impulsive emotion.

Day 14: Serving Others The antidote to self-absorption and overwhelming grief is choosing to **serve someone else**, especially those who cannot repay you.

Key Point: **Pure religion** is to visit the fatherless and widows in their distress (James 1:27).

Key Action: Shift your daily focus from **worry** (which drains) to **purpose** (which fills) by finding a cause to serve.

Day 15: Empathy Offering **empathy** (shared understanding) to others who walk a similar path is far more powerful than receiving general sympathy.

Key Point: We are comforted in our trouble so that we can **comfort others** (2 Corinthians 1:3–4).

Key Action: Turn the temptation to compare your pain into a means of **connecting** with another suffering parent.

Day 16: Vulnerability True strength is found in honest weakness. **Vulnerability**—sharing your struggle with a trusted, safe person—allows God's power to work through you.

Key Point: God's **power is perfected in weakness** (2 Corinthians 12:9).

Key Action: Identify your **safe person** and commit to being fully honest with them, allowing them to carry the load with you.

Day 17: Influence .vs Control You must redefine your role. **Control** (dictating the outcome) belongs to God. Your job is **influence** through prayer, love, and a steady example.

Key Point: Trying to control your adult child only pushes them further away. Respect their **free will**.

Key Action: Embrace the **Influence of Peace**—your stability is a more powerful beacon than any argument or manipulation.

Day 18: God's Promises God's promises are the **unshakable guarantees** you must cling to when your circumstances feel fluid and uncertain. They are anchors for your soul.

Key Point: The **Promiser is faithful** (Hebrews 10:23). Your confidence is in Him, not the signs you see.

Key Action: Identify and write out three or four **specific promises** you will pray over your child daily (e.g., Proverbs 22:6).

Day 19: God's Comfort When you are exhausted and despairing, stop striving and allow yourself to be held by the **God of all comfort**.

Key Point: He gathers the lambs in His arms and **gently leads** those with young (Isaiah 40:11).

Key Action: Give yourself permission to **rest** and receive God's comfort, acknowledging that rest is not failure.

Day 20: Trusting God The ultimate act of surrender is to completely hand over the burden of your child and the crisis to God. This total reliance is the only way to find freedom.

Key Point: **Cast all your anxiety on Him, because He cares for you** (1 Peter 5:7, NASB).

Key Action: **Hurl** the burden of your current anxiety onto God right now and trust that He will sustain you.

Day 21: Hope: Hope is not wishful thinking; it is the **certainty** of God's redemptive plan. It anchors your soul in the knowledge that God finishes what He starts.

Key Point: **Hope does not disappoint** (Romans 5:5, NASB). God is faithful to His own nature.

Key Action: Actively look for small **glimmers of grace** in your daily life to reinforce the bigger hope.

Day 22: When the answer is no It's essential to wrestle honestly with God about the pain and the delay, but you must not let your wrestling become **resentment** of His plan.

Key Point: The "no" or "wait" is meant to perfect His power in your weakness: **"My grace is sufficient"** (2 Corinthians 12:9).

Key Action: End your wrestling in surrender: **"Not My will, but Yours be done"** (Luke 22:42).

Day 23: Your Role Once your child is an adult, you must accept that you are their parent forever, but you are their protector never. Your old job was to ensure their safety and make their decisions; your new job is to influence through prayer, love, and a steady example. You must define a new role with healthy boundaries.

Key Point: Stop trying to be their God or their savior. Your child is an adult and **responsible for their own choices** (Galatians 6:5).

Key Action: Clearly define what you will and will not do (e.g., will love them unconditionally, will not enable the addiction). You must love them from a distance of healthy boundaries.

Day 24: Marathon This journey is a **spiritual marathon**, not a sprint. You must pace yourself for the long haul and manage your energy to avoid burnout and collapse.

Key Point: **"Run with endurance the race that is set before us"** (Hebrews 12:1).

Key Action: Lay aside the encumbrance (heavy baggage of guilt or control) and prioritize spiritual **self-care**.

Day 25: Timing God's delay is never accidental; it is His **patience**. He is waiting for the perfect, appointed moment for maximum depth and redemption in their life.

Key Point: God is the patient farmer (James 5:7). He cannot rush the harvest.

Key Action: Use the waiting time for **active expectation** (looking for God to move), not passive worry.

Day 26: Why Pray Prayer is not a duty or a last resort; it is the **channel of God's peace**. It is how you engage God's will and receive strength for the day.

Key Point: Through prayer, your requests are made known to God, and His **peace** will guard you (Philippians 4:6-7).

Key Action: Turn your anxious worry into a **focused prayer** immediately upon feeling the anxiety rising.

Day 27: When to Pray You need both **scheduled discipline** (crying to God day and night) and **spontaneous reliance** (praying without ceasing) that turns every moment into a conversation.

Key Point: **"Pray without ceasing"** (1 Thessalonians 5:17, NASB).

Key Action: Establish a set time for structured prayer and commit to several **pop-up prayers** throughout the day.

Day 28: How to Pray The most powerful way to pray is by aligning your words with God's will—**praying Scripture**. This provides confidence and spiritual authority.

Key Point: When you pray the Word, you are confident you are asking according to God's **will** (1 John 5:14).

Key Action: Begin using the **50 Scriptures** chapter as a template for your daily prayer life.

Day 29: Where to Pray Be intentional about choosing your prayer spots: your **personal sanctuary**, your **corporate sanctuary** (church), and the **battlefield** (praying on the spot).

Key Point: When two or three are gathered, Christ is **in the midst** (Matthew 18:20).

Key Action: Seek out a faithful prayer partner to meet with regularly and intercede together.

Day 30: Forgiveness: Forgiveness is a conscious, spiritual decision for your own freedom. You must release the debt of resentment to free yourself, regardless of your child's repentance.

Key Point: Forgive each other, just as **God in Christ also has forgiven you** (Ephesians 4:32, NASB).

Key Action: **Cast the debt** onto God, releasing your right to hold the wrong against them.

Day 31: Your Identity Your worth is **not** determined by your child's choices or your parenting outcome. Your identity is found entirely in your position as a **child of God**.

Key Point: You are **chosen, holy, and beloved** (Colossians 3:12, NASB).

Key Action: Stop looking at the "cracked mirror" of circumstance and rest in the truth of your **fixed value** in Christ.

Final Thoughts

First, thank you so much for taking the time to read this book. It is my prayer that this has been a blessing to you and your family.

Secondly, if you have an opportunity to send me an e-mail with your thoughts, comments, or suggestions, that would be very helpful.

Finally, I hope you were encouraged and strengthened by what you read.

paulbeersdorf@gmail.com

Blessings to you and your family!

Paul Beersdorf

www.ingramcontent.com/pod-product-compliance
Lightning Source LLC
Chambersburg PA
CBHW060318050426
42449CB00011B/2536